PREVENTING
WORKPLACE
VIOLENCE

Advanced Topics in Organizational Behavior

The **Advanced Topics in Organizational Behavior** series examines current and emerging issues in the field of organizational behavior. Written by researchers who are widely acknowledged subject area experts, the books provide an authoritative, up-to-date review of the conceptual, research, and practical implications of the major issues in organizational behavior.

PREVENTING
WORKPLACE
VIOLENCE

A Guide
for
Employers
and
Practitioners

MARK BRAVERMAN

SAGE Publications
International Educational and Professional Publisher
Thousand Oaks   London   New Delhi

For information:

SAGE Publications, Inc.
2455 Teller Road
Thousand Oaks, California 91320
E-mail: order@sagepub.com

SAGE Publications Ltd.
6 Bonhill Street
London EC2A 4PU
United Kingdom

SAGE Publications India Pvt. Ltd.
M-32 Market
Greater Kailash I
New Delhi 110 048 India

Printed in the United States of America

Library of Congress Cataloging-in-Publication Data

Braverman, Mark.
    Preventing workplace violence: A guide for employers and
practitioners / by Mark Braverman.
        p.   cm.—(Advanced topics in organizational behavior)
    Includes bibliographical references and index.
    ISBN 0-7619-0614-2 (acid-free paper)
    ISBN 0-7619-0615-0 (pbk.: acid-free paper)
    1. Violence in the workplace—Prevention. I. Title. II. Series.
    HF5549.5.E43 B73   1999
    658.4'73—dc21   98-40177

This book is printed on acid-free paper.

99   00   01   02   03   04   05   7   6   5   4   3   2   1

Acquiring Editor:	Marquita Flemming
Editorial Assistant:	MaryAnn Vail
Production Editor:	Denise Santoyo
Production Assistant:	Stephanie Allen
Typesetter:	Lynn Miyata
Cover Designer:	Candice Harman

To the memory of my father,
Samuel Braverman
1917-1998

The memory of a righteous man
is a blessing.

Contents

Acknowledgments

Many people and experiences went into the making of this book. Dr. Bessel van der Kolk, my teacher and mentor, now colleague and friend, was my guide to understanding the effects of extreme stress on human beings. Bessel also taught me, as he has so many others in our field, to push hard against the established assumptions of mental health theory and practice. His questioning, iconoclastic spirit continues to influence me. I owe much to several colleagues in psychology: Dr. Steven White, a pioneer and innovator in the assessment of violence in a workplace context, was a valued colleague and collaborator. I have been honored to be able to call on Drs. John Daignault and Robert Fein for advice and direction over the years. They have taught me much about the causes of violent behavior. Robert Fein critiqued sections of the manuscript and has been a generous colleague over the years, particularly on the issue of violence prediction.

A fundamental discovery that inspired this book is that the understanding of workplace violence requires the integration of several fields. Richard and Tia Denenberg are the moving forces behind Workplace Solutions, the nonprofit we established with them in 1997 to promote violence prevention and collaborative problem solving in the workplace. Experts in dispute resolution and labor relations, possessed of searching intellects and big hearts, Dick and Tia are valued colleagues and an inspiration for my continual exploration of the boundaries of this work.

My friend and colleague Dr. Julian Barling, coeditor of this series, first suggested that I write this book and has been a wonderful support throughout the process. Julian, together with Drs. Wayne Corneil and Kevin Kelloway, provided a thorough review of the manuscript and valuable suggestions for its improvement. Marquita Flemming of Sage Publications has made the publication process a delight. I am grateful to MaryAnn Vail of Sage for her tireless and skilled work in turning the manuscript into a finished product and for her patience through multiple revisions of the text.

Susan Braverman, my wife and my partner in our work together for over 20 years, has seen me through this project, as she has so many others, with patience, love, and the more-than-occasional push. In addition to her critical and editing skills, Susan has always provided the support and the ground for my best efforts. My appreciation goes to Susan, along with Dr. Bruce Cedar, our partner at CMG Associates, who together shouldered more than their share of the workload of our consulting firm in the critical weeks and months approaching several deadlines.

My 13-year-old son Jacob, a gifted writer, provided incisive editing and suggestions for several chapters. I have appreciated his support, interest, and encouragement, despite his occasional cries of "When are you going to write some fiction, Dad?"

Finally, thanks go to the countless employees, managers, and union officials whose experiences have provided the lessons I have endeavored to convey in this book. Their struggles, their failures, their triumphs, and, most of all, their willingness to learn are the heart and the hope for a more humane, healthy, and safe working environment.

Preface

Violence in the workplace is a hot issue. In the United States, the federal government has officially recognized violence as a workplace hazard and has directed employers to take precautions (National Institute for Occupational Safety and Health, 1993). Statistics are often cited in discussions about this topic, but, not surprisingly, the numbers are prone to distortion and misinterpretation. Indisputably, the rate of homicide in the U.S. workplace is shockingly high: Government data for 1980 through 1988 place homicide as the third leading cause of death at work, at 17% (Jenkins, Layne, & Kisner, 1992). These data, however, are often misunderstood to refer to violence committed *by employees toward fellow employees*. In fact, employee-on-employee homicide occurring at work accounts for only 4% to 7% of violence-related deaths at work. The remainder of the homicides are related to robberies and other crimes (Toscano & Weber, 1995). Nonfatal violence, including assaults and threats, is harder to quantify. One widely quoted source indicates that the rate of nonfatal assault or threat in the United States may be as high as 25% (Northwest National Life Insurance Company, 1993). A survey of Canadian public employees found that over 60% had experienced at least one incident of violence or threatened violence ("CUPE Survey," 1993). (The Canadian study, however, does not indicate the sources of the violence.)

Media attention has amplified the hysteria and controversy surrounding the topic, contributing to the focus on the rare but newsworthy incidents of coworker mayhem. Consultants and trainers attuned to the latest marketing opportunities have produced mountains of videos, workbooks, and manuals. Law firms offer seminars to educate employers on how to protect themselves from liability from violence-related injuries and how to legally pursue possible threat scenarios.[1] On the industrial relations front, employers and unions argue about who is to blame for this increase in the climate of violence in today's workplaces.

Despite the media and marketplace-fueled confusion surrounding the topic, business leaders have seized on this issue, clamoring for programs and procedures that can provide protection against this perceived threat. This is because, regardless of any distortion or misunderstanding of the actual statistical risks, the people on the front line—that is, those responsible for the safety and health of the workplace—understand the costs of threats, assaults, and fear on the morale and productivity of their employees. They also understand the costs of negative publicity, bad public relations, and litigation on the survival of their enterprises. Violence in the workplace, whether it comes from the outside or originates from within, is a frightening prospect.

The prevention of violence affecting workers is one of the most important policy issues facing the workplace today. A central thesis of the book is that the standard, traditional tools for occupational health and safety, discipline, and employee relations now used by business and labor leaders are inadequate and inappropriate for responding to the problem of workplace violence. In fact, the methods and approaches commonly in use actually worsen the problem in some cases. To effectively confront the violence issue, business and labor leaders must deal with a range of crucial workplace issues, including the following.

> *The limits of our present concepts about worker rights and employer responsibility.* Time-honored principles of employment law such as the duty to protect occupational health and safety, workers' rights to privacy, and protection from discrimination have shaped employment policy and practice. Unfortunately, they have also created a dispute-centered, adversarial context that is highly hazardous in its own right. In union as well as nonunion environments, increased stresses on employees and organizations have created an urgent need for alternative methods of dispute resolution and conflict management. The violence issue may present one of the best opportunities in decades for this work to move forward.

The limits of our current human resources practices. Dealing with threats of violence from both within and outside of the workplace challenges what we know about best practice in handling issues of interemployee conflict, impaired workers, and actual threats and acts of violence. Repeatedly, human resource managers, sometimes in concert with internal security or legal departments, stumble in trying to deal with these complex and frightening situations. When they do turn to outside professionals for help, whether these are in the mental health, legal, or mediation fields, it is often too late to reverse the damage.

The limits of current occupational health and disability policies and procedures. Violent or threatening employees almost always interact with the occupational health system, whether on their own or through the intervention of management. These systems are not equipped to address the suffering or desperation of these employees or to provide useful information or guidance for the concerned employer. Because of the increase in job stress due to structural and economic changes in the workplace and fundamental changes in health care policy and delivery, it is crucial that we examine the role of health care and disability policy in the handling of workplace violence.

Health, safety, and labor relations. Finally, workplace violence episodes bring to the surface crucial issues of industrial labor relations and have implications for the legal, labor relations, dispute mediation, and health professions. Health and safety in the workplace can no longer be the province of midlevel managers responding to government regulations and compliance standards. They can no longer be a battleground between labor and management. The issues have broadened beyond the traditional categories of equipment and environmental hazards. Safety and health now have to do with the greatly increased stress brought on by fundamental changes in the structure of work and work roles and shifts in the employment contract. These changes have increased the performance pressure, economic insecurity, and potential for conflict and competition among workers. They have disrupted crucial structures of trust and communication. The question now facing our society is nothing less than this: Can we preserve our workplaces as places fit for people? Now, more than ever in our history, it is crucial for leadership of industry and those representing the labor force to come together and confront these risks.

The purpose of this book is to describe the phenomenon of workplace violence through a number of representative cases and to present a practical guide for those involved in responding to this threat to the health and safety of our workplaces. In Chapters 1 through 3, I will present the concepts and issues that we need to understand in order to confront the phenomenon of workplace violence: What is workplace violence? How can violence be understood in the context of the changes and crises faced by the workplace? Chapters 4 through 8 are case histories. They provide a detailed look at what has happened to some companies and individuals who have been caught up in this complex issue. The final chapters are intended to be a practical guide for the employer, manager, union leader, and consultant. In these chapters, I summarize the learning from the case histories and offer my recommendations for the future direction of workplace violence prevention.

Note

1. Not all the advice is helpful. Chapter 9 of this book takes up this topic in detail.

1

Show Me the Profile:

A Day in the Life of a Violence Consultant

We would rather be ruined than changed,
We would rather die in our dread
Than climb the cross of the moment
And let our illusions die.

W. H. Auden, *The Age of Anxiety*

The call comes in almost weekly. "This is Bob Smith of ABC Corporation. I'm in charge of health and safety (or human resources, or training). We want to implement a violence prevention program." Requests such as this are usually welcomed by those of us who have done our share of crisis intervention. Prevention is hard to come by in a society where crisis intervention has always meant "cleanup" rather than help in preventing disasters. But what usually follows in these conversations is far from comforting. "Bob" continues with the following request: "We want you to train our supervisors in how to recognize dangerous or violent employees: You know, the profile."

The Profile

So many of us can recite the list: "a white male, in his 40s or 50s, divorced or separated, a loner with an interest in guns." You can find this description in numerous books and articles written about workplace violence since the topic appeared on our collective radar screen in the late 1980s. Training in the profile purports to alert supervisory, safety, and human resources personnel to the signs that an employee may pose a threat to fellow workers or superiors. It is often invoked in cases where someone is to be terminated or laid off. The profile also turns up in another common request: "How can we screen out violent people in the hiring process?"

The concept of the profile is highly problematic. It raises a host of scientific, clinical, legal, and ethical issues. But that is not what makes me so uncomfortable with "the call." What really bothers me is that what is being requested is not going to provide even a modicum of violence prevention. As this book will describe in detail, preventing violence in the workplace involves much more than trying to spot those among your employees who may have violent tendencies. There are several things wrong with this preoccupation with the profile.

First, the "revenge killing" scenario that so concerns employers, although understandably frightening, makes up only a small part of the full scope of workplace violence. Vastly more people are threatened, beaten up, or seriously harassed at work than are ever gunned down. Furthermore, when we do look at the workplace homicide statistics, national statistics for the United States show that barely 4% of people murdered at work are killed by another employee! (Toscano & Weber, 1995). Rather, the fatalities stem overwhelmingly from assaults on workers by criminals from outside the workplace, usually in armed robberies on late-night retail establishments, or on taxicab drivers. For women, the statistics show us clearly that most women murdered at work are the victims of domestic violence or stalking scenarios. So even though the "disgruntled worker" scenario grabs the headlines, it is a very small part of the problem. Focusing on this small sector of the phenomenon does not address the preponderance of the harm to employees resulting from violence at work.

Second, profiling is not practical. The profile itself is too broad compared to how rare the event is: What, precisely, do you *do* once you have identified all the socially isolated divorced white males in your workforce who are preoccupied with guns and tend to blame other people for their problems? Also, information about a history of violent behavior is either unavailable or hard to come by for the employer. Even if you can reliably obtain a criminal record for an applicant, most perpetrators of workplace violence do not carry felony convictions, so you cannot screen them on that basis.[1]

Third, the experts on prediction do not talk about a profile. They do look at personality issues, but only in the context of the precipitating situation, other stresses on the person, the actual context in which the threat is made, the availability of weapons, and the actual behavior that gives rise to the concerns about violence. A review of the academic and professional literature on the prediction of violence reveals no mention of a "profile" (Fein, Vossekuil, & Holden, 1995; Monahan, 1981). Rather, it comes up in the books, pamphlets, training workbooks, and videos that are marketed to the business community.

Finally, this preoccupation with "revenge killings" at work is the worst kind of blind alley. Focusing on individuals who may be at risk for violence on the basis of lists of characteristics alone is useless as a predictive tool and illegal in almost all cases from an employment law standpoint. Most important, however, limiting the focus to a search for predictive tools is a dangerous distraction from the crucial issues raised when we take a look at the real causes of the workplace violence problem.

So why this interest in the profile?

1. Our culture, and certainly our training in many of our jobs, has taught us to look for neat, simple solutions to complex problems. We are hungry for easy, "cookie cutter" answers. Especially in these days of daily crises and tight budgets, the push is for quick solutions so that we can get on to the next crisis.

2. We want to know who the "bad guys" are. We search for places to put the blame for the rage and unhappiness that is infecting our workplaces. More than anything, we want to put distance between ourselves and the feeling of loss of control that we feel as we watch our assumptions about work and the employment relationship be swept away in wave after wave of organizational changes.

3. We deny the importance of a sense of community in our workplaces. Rapid change within the workplace and in society can produce a breakdown in the essential connections and sense of trust between people. This creates scapegoating and the abuse of power: When people feel frightened, they look for objects of blame. However, the cure for fear is not blame, it is the repair of the broken connections between the people that make up an organization. As we shall see when we discuss the causes of violence in Chapter 3, the conflict, threat, intimidation, and out-of-control behavior in our midst are engendered by a climate of isolation, alienation, mistrust, and helplessness. The demographics of the workforce and the personality characteristics of individuals are just part of the mix.

Our caller's request revealed a powerful and dangerous assumption: that the threat of violence in the workplace is located within a specific group of people and that by somehow uncovering who they are we will be safe from that threat. As we will see from the cases to be presented in this book, this is far from the reality confronted by those responsible for maintaining a climate of health, safety, and creativity in our workplaces. Anyone who has ever had to manage crises concerning human behavior in the workplace knows that the causes of violence lie as much in our systems as they do in the people themselves. The keys to prevention are to be found in the systems we construct to deal with a host of human issues that arise at work and in the values and commitment that we bring to the implementation of those systems, policies, and procedures.

What kind of human environment are we creating in our places of employment? The workplace is a microcosm of our society, and the issue of how we perceive and confront the problem of violence at work crystallizes and focuses a host of questions that are crucial to our society as a whole. Western society is engaged in a struggle against the poisonous influence of materialism. Materialism dictates that what matters is things, not people. It engenders what Max DePree (1989) called "exclusiveness," the kind of driven selfishness that distances us from our feelings of compassion and connection to others. It can infect our conduct as managers and coworkers. Under its influence, we reduce violence to a list of traits and descriptors, rather than understanding it as the story of actual people coping with real conditions. What we learn from the cases to be presented in this book is that an act of violence, whether in word or deed, is the outcome of a *process.* Solving the problem requires no less than an examination of the process by which we treat our fellow human beings in the community of the workplace.

Examining this process means looking at the policies that we create to ensure safety and fairness at work. As we will see, how policies are constructed and applied is a barometer of the health of the workplace. The current preoccupation with workplace violence has created a flurry of policy-producing activity in companies across North America. But policies applied in an atmosphere of mistrust and alienation can become the tools of scapegoating and denial.[2] Policies adopted without the commitment of people in positions of leadership and without the assurance of collaboration and communication can result in costly and even tragic disasters. As we study the cases to follow, we will see just how destructive it can be when employers use a hasty, fragmented approach to this issue. In short, to paraphrase that famous statement of the cartoon character Pogo, we will search in vain for the enemy until we realize that "it is us."

Notes

1. Experts question the common wisdom that a history of violence is a reliable predictor of violence potential. Chapter 3 provides a more detailed discussion of this issue.

2. DePree (1989, p. 112) listed "manuals" as a primary sign of organizational entropy: the fatal loss of values and direction in an organization.

2

The Crisis of Work

Managers in crisis-prepared organizations have learned this fundamental lesson: crisis management concerns the totality of their organization . . . and is an expression of the organization's fundamental purpose or strategic vision.

T. Pauchant and I. Mitroff,
Transforming the Crisis-Prone Organization

Corporations, like the people who compose them, are always in a state of becoming.

Max DePree, *Leadership Is an Art*

At the heart of this book are the stories of people whose lives have been disrupted by workplace violence. As you enter with me into these cases, however, you will understand what I saw when I first began this work over 10 years ago: Under the surface of these episodes of workplace violence, there is a much bigger story. It is the story of what happens when the workplace turns into a pressure cooker of stress that threatens to destroy the health and in some cases the lives of working people. In the chapters to follow, you will read about some of the causes of this stress: unions and company management embattled and mistrustful; human resources and employee relations departments overwhelmed by the demands of unrelenting organizational change; murderous domestic violence spilling into the workplace. These stories afford a look into environments of competition and uncertainty that set people against one another, push many past their limits, and, for many workers, have turned the workplace into a place of desperation, isolation, and despair.

The Nature of the Crisis in the American Workplace

Paul Shrivastava (1992), Professor of Management at Bucknell University and an innovator in the emerging field of crisis management, provided a powerful description of the current state of our world: "We live in a crisis-prone and crisis-laden world—a world in which crises are omnipresent and proliferating. Every aspect of society faces damaging disruptions, upheaval and restructuring, which are the hallmarks of crises." In Shrivastava's analysis, crisis is global. It is reflected at every level of society, including the modern corporation. Talk to any CEO, human resources director, safety and health manager, or head of an operational unit in virtually any industry today, and he or she will confirm this view. In Shrivastava's view, however, this condition is not cause for despair. The corporations that are going to survive and prosper are those that recognize crises as opportunities for positive and important change, rather than as unpleasant disruptions that threaten the status quo and should be avoided. "Sustainable corporations," he wrote, are companies that are open to constant change and restructuring. The extent to which corporations recognize and respond to these crises will determine how well a company is prepared for the crises it will face.

In a similar vein, Pauchant and Mitroff (1992), two writers who have also studied the way crises have affected modern corporations, offered a compelling model in which they contrasted the "crisis-prone" and the "crisis-prepared" organization. Focusing on the proliferation of human and environmental crises that characterize modern society, they argued that corporations that deny the possibility of crisis inevitably expose themselves to the most severe and potentially disastrous situations:

> Managers in crisis-prepared organizations have learned this fundamental lesson: *crisis management concerns the totality of their organization . . . and is an*

expression of the organization's fundamental purpose or strategic vision [italics added]. . . . If an organization is not positioned well with regard to crisis management, then it is probably not well positioned to compete successfully in the new global economy. (p. 126)

Like Shrivastava, these writers held that the concept of crisis is crucial for an understanding of the challenges facing the modern corporation. They saw the growing global crisis reflected in the novel, complex situations that are faced at a constantly increasing rate by managers in companies and work organizations of all kinds. Furthermore, they agreed that the solutions are social, not technological:

The sociotechnical systems that we call "corporations" are so complex and interdependent that they have become extremely fragile. . . . A minor event, even a single individual, can now have a drastic effect on an organization as a whole and on its community and environment. These events will not diminish in this century; they are, in fact, increasing rapidly. (p. 126)

This quote sums up a fundamental leadership and management issue of this decade, and one that will drive the search for workable solutions into the next century. Crises are no longer isolated, episodic events in the life of a company. Rather, they have to do with complex and "nontechnological" issues such as stress, communication, trust, flexibility, and caring. Furthermore, crisis management is not something that can be pigeonholed as the responsibility of a single function such as safety, corporate communications, legal, or human resources. Dealing with crises has become the daily occupation of managers at all levels and functions. Today, a key leadership capability is the capacity to understand the inevitability of crisis and to be prepared for it.

Leadership and Crisis Management: Beyond Public Relations

The term *crisis management* was invented by the public relations industry. There, it is used to describe the manipulation of public and stockholder opinion in the midst of a corporate disaster or scandal such as product contamination; environmental, industrial, or transportation disaster; or employer misconduct. Well-known examples include the Bhopal India chemical spill, the *Exxon Valdez* oil spill, the Tylenol tamperings, the recent crashes of ValueJet and TWA flights, the *Challenger* space shuttle explosion, and the racial discrimination suit against

Texaco. These events all had the potential to threaten the very existence of the corporations and agencies that presided over them. The way they were handled (or mishandled) by the leadership at the time had profound consequences for the recovery of the organization.

But corporate crises are not limited to disasters that cause mass casualties, widespread environmental damage, or two-inch headlines. Crises come to the attention of corporate executives, human resource managers, safety directors, corporate lawyers, and risk managers on a weekly, if not daily, basis. What I have learned over the years, and what has taken the field of crisis management beyond the opinion and "spin control" activities of the public relations industry, is one simple fact: Crises have a profound effect on employees. These effects extend beyond the immediate circle of victims. They involve the health, productivity, loyalty, morale, and even employment longevity of employees from the line level through middle and upper management. Having systems in place to handle the *internal* effects of crisis has become the responsibility of companies large and small, public and private, white and blue collar (Braverman, 1992). Unions, too, are staking out new territory in crisis management. Progressive forces in several labor organizations are realizing that protecting workers from the damaging and sometimes fatal effects of crises at work will have to be a central feature of labor's role into the next century (Barab, 1996b).

Crisis Prepared or Crisis Prone?

Pauchant and Mitroff (1992) used the terms *crisis prone* and *crisis prepared* to differentiate between companies that have recognized the reality of crisis and those that, at their peril, have not. They developed their model from studying major disasters such as the ones cited above. However, what they described applies equally to the "crisis" of workplace violence, as we shall see from the cases to be presented here. At the center of Pauchant and Mitroff's model is the importance of early detection of and response to warning signals. The ability to listen and take action is the difference between *reactive* and *proactive* crisis management, as illustrated in Figure 2.1.

Traditionally, crisis management has existed solely on the *reactive* side of this model. The crisis occurs: A system malfunctions, causing death or injury; an employee "blows a whistle" on a scandalous or illegal internal practice; a flawed or dangerous product is suddenly exposed; a disturbed, unhappy employee threatens or commits violence. The organization responds with the first reactive stage:

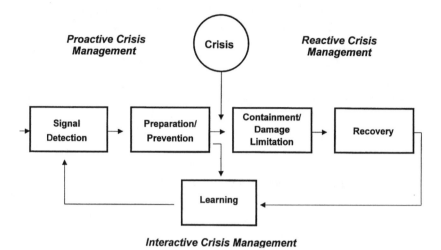

Figure 2.1. Phases of Crisis Management
SOURCE: From Pauchant and Mitroff (1992).

damage control. This usually involves engaging in public relations activity to protect the image of the company, finding people to blame, and punishing them. The final stage of reactive crisis management is *recovery.* In the reactive mode, recovery almost always means an official covering up or denial of the real meaning of the crisis or disaster: "It was the fault of a single individual. He is gone now, so we'll be fine." "This was a fluke. Things like this don't really happen to us. It won't happen again." The effect of this reactive mode of behavior is to block any learning or change that might come as the result of the crisis.[1]

Organizations develop the capacity for proactive crisis management by learning from experience. A look at Figure 2.1 shows that when a company moves past damage control and recovery into a willingness to learn from the crisis, it will discover that there were warning signs and clear antecedents to the trouble. As we will see in the cases to follow, these signs may point to problematic individual behavior as well as to flawed organizational systems. Becoming crisis prepared means developing the means to detect and respond to these signals. More important, it means preserving the ability to continue to learn from subsequent crises so that the ability to detect and respond proactively continues to develop and expand. In fact, learning becomes a part of the organization's developing culture.

The Learning Organization:
Systems Theory and Workplace Violence

Pauchant and Mitroff's work on reactive and proactive crisis management is an example of systems thinking. Some of the most influential work on business and management in the past decade has come from systems theory and its proponents. Systems thinking bears directly on the issue of violence and the crises that surround threat and violent behavior in the workplace.

Peter Senge's *The Fifth Discipline* (1990) introduced a generation of managers to systems thinking. In his description of the "learning organization," Senge explained that for any business to function successfully, its leaders must understand that every act has an effect on every other act and that each organizational function is part of an interconnected system. In a learning organization, people strive to understand why something has gone wrong by looking at the entire interconnected system of events and decisions. In contrast, in a poorly functioning organization, every misfortune or setback is followed by a search for someone or something to blame. The assumption is that a single act or decision is responsible for the disaster. For example, after the *Exxon Valdez* oil spill, one dysfunctional response was to blame the captain of the ship; speculation abounded that he was drunk at the time of the accident. The corporation could just as easily have targeted for blame the person or persons who made the decision to use a shipping channel that was too narrow or the decision to use a single-hulled ship despite safety warnings. In fact, a systems thinking approach would suggest that the disaster happened only because *all* of these conditions were met. In a systems-thinking analysis, one would examine the faulty systems for communication, prevention, and decision making that allowed these conditions to prevail. A more recent example of the failure to apply a systems approach is provided by the series of shocking killings by teenagers in U.S. public schools in 1998. The shootings were followed immediately by cries for tougher gun control, with the president himself leading the charge. This was followed by numerous pronouncements about the effects of media violence. Few, if any, voices were heard proposing a study of the flawed systems in the communities and schools that allowed clear warning signals to go unrecognized.

The classic example of unheeded warning signals is the space shuttle *Challenger* disaster. After the tragedy, it became known that warnings from several sources about faulty design and the dangers of launching in cold weather were ignored or blocked (Pauchant & Mitroff, 1992). Crisis-prone organizations face a "double jeopardy": First, the lack of systems thinking allows for poor risk management because no one is looking at the whole picture. It is as if all the pieces of the puzzle are lying on the table, but no one thinks to assemble them. Mounting evidence of unacceptable risk or explosive conditions can literally be rendered invisible in this way. Second, this same lack of coordination allows even the clearest, most alarming signals to be silenced because there is little communication or accountability.

Like Pauchant and Mitroff, Senge (1990) argued that systems break down and crises occur precisely because those responsible for planning and decision making do not recognize or understand the complexity that underlies any event or phenomenon. Senge would agree that attempts to resolve crises on the basis of nonsystems thinking lead to an often disastrous worsening of the crisis. "The cure," he wrote, "can be worse than the disease" (p. 61). In Senge's view, faulty, non-system-level approaches on the part of managers lead directly to business crises. These principles bear directly on the issue of violence in the workplace.

In the chapters to follow, we will see how a fragmented approach to decision making and crisis management plays a major role in a wide range of workplace violence phenomena. We will see how multiple systems such as discipline, occupational health and disability, security, and labor relations fail to respond effectively to reports of violence-related threats. We will see how the sources of stress leading to violence are not considered when plans or policies to prevent violence in the workplace are developed. We will see how impaired or innocent employees are hurt or victimized because of systems that overreact or respond with well-intentioned but deeply flawed actions: "The cure is worse than the disease."

Violence as Crisis

Every act of violence is the result of a series of events. Referring to Figure 2.1, we see that, like all crises, every situation involving a threat or act of violence is preceded by early signs of trouble. The signals are as varied as the systems and levels that make up every workplace. The signs may be on a system level, such as high levels of grievances, indicating poor morale or labor-management conflict; incidents of assaults or threats from clients or customers; or requests for increased security on entering or leaving the facility at night. The sign may involve a single employee who has submitted a claim for stress, complained of harassment, or reported domestic abuse. A crisis-prone organization will allow these early signs of possible violence or conflict to go undetected. If the company leadership responds at all to danger signals, it will typically allow them to be handled by standard disciplinary, labor relations, security, or occupational health systems. Only when the crisis has blown up will it take direct action.

The Sources of Stress

The sources of the stress on organizational systems are multiple and complex. They originate from the work situation itself as well as from outside the work environment in the community and the family. The causes of workplace violence range from the continuing stress of organizational restructuring, to an accident that kills, sickens, or maims, to an episode or pattern of abuse or harassment. Leaders in crisis-prepared organizations understand that stress that directly affects the people in their companies can come from any of the following sources and will have a direct impact on the health of their people and the success of their business. Crisis-prepared businesses will have systems to alert them to such danger signs as the following:

- There are *conflicts between employees,* including harassment, fights, threats, or severe breakdown in work group functioning.
- Conflicts are emerging from the *increasing diversity* of the workforce. These can result in sexual harassment allegations and discrimination claims.
- Crises of morale, productivity, and even safety inevitably arise in the midst of a *downsizing or restructuring.* The relentless pace of change, both inside the workplace and in society at large, continues to create stress and disruption that affect individuals and the work organizations they inhabit. The loss of job security for employees at all levels, together with greatly increased performance pressure, causes stress levels to reach the breaking point for many employees, creating mounting concerns about violence and conflict within the workplace.
- Managers and safety and health personnel frequently confront confusing, complex and often frightening workplace issues involving *drug and alcohol abuse* and *domestic violence.*
- *Mental health and behavior problems* create concerns about safety daily in work-places. As stress increases, both at home and at an ever-changing workplace, instances of unstable and problematic behavior increase.
- Employees in *high-risk industries* such as retail, transportation, and health care suffer high rates of fatal and nonfatal assault and threat at the hands of criminals, patients, and customers.

The Need for Connection

Concern for the distress of potentially dangerous people does not translate to "coddling" the offender or being "soft on crime." Rather, it has to do with giving managers the proper tools to deal with disruptive and potentially dangerous situations. You cannot change economic realities or give someone a better home life. But the employment relationship provides a context in which the prepared, properly equipped employer can act effectively to evaluate and resolve the threat to safety or health. By honoring and utilizing the connection that exists with each employee, the employer is making use of the most valuable and effective tool available to prevent and stop the damage of violence in the workplace.

A workplace can thrive only when its members feel positively connected to one another and when employees at all levels feel trusting toward the organization as a whole. These qualities are threatened by traumas such as a downsizing, a fatal accident, or an intentional or negligent abuse of power. The very survival of a company is threatened when leaders ignore or deny the powerful effects of such events. Whereas members of a workforce can understand the need for change, and even the inevitability of mistakes or accidents that cause death or injury, they cannot long tolerate alienation and lack of connectedness. When change and trauma are handled incorrectly, people at all levels of the organization become nervous, unsure of their footing and of their interdependent relation to others in the structure. Crucial breakdowns in trust and communication begin to occur. Time and again, we hear from managers in such an environment that they feel unsupported by and out of contact with their superiors. They feel the faltering of leadership acutely. Fearful for their own positions, they become afraid to speak up about conditions or situations that concern them. People suffer in silence rather than reaching out for help. Managers and supervisors hide worrisome or explosive situations rather than bringing them to the attention of superiors. Without trust in the system, people do not communicate. Without communication, there is no early warning, and no opportunity to take steps to correct what is wrong.

Violence at work therefore occurs in the context of the larger system. The severe stresses affecting the modern workplace manifest directly in system-level crises involving breakdowns in communication between line staff and management, loss of morale and loyalty to the company, and the failure of systems designed to deal with conflict resolution, fairness, and physical security itself. On an individual level, increasing alienation, stress, and helplessness lead inevitably to dysfunctional, disruptive, and even dangerous behavior. You can prevent violence only by confronting these phenomena on a system level, and only if you are on the "proactive" side of the crisis management chart. That is why, for example, the focus on the "profile" of the dangerous employee is such an inadequate and self-defeating strategy.

That said, however, it is still important to understand what causes some people to become violent. Who is this violent employee that our society is so concerned about? We take up this question in the next chapter.

Note

1. Pauchant and Mitroff (1992) offered a comprehensive and excellent discussion of the forms of institutional denial and self-delusion in the face of crisis.

3

Who Is the
Violent Employee?

Our age is an era of radical transition. The old myths and symbols by
which we oriented ourselves are gone, anxiety is rampant. . . .The
individual . . . becomes obsessed with the new problem of identity,
namely, Even-if-I-know-who-I-am, I-have-no-significance. . . . The
next step is apathy. And the step following that is violence. For no
human being can stand the perpetually numbing experience of his
own powerlessness.

Rollo May, *Love and Will*

The employee who becomes the focus of concern about violence potential is
someone who is at risk. He or she may be someone who copes poorly with
stress, has a history of violent behavior, or maintains poor interpersonal relationships. Who is this person? What, if any, is the responsibility of the workplace for

generating this risk of violence, and what is the possibility that this same system can defuse the violence brewing within its ranks?

Before taking on the question of the violent employee, it is important to remind ourselves that interemployee violence is only part of the total workplace violence picture. The California Occupational Safety and Health Administration (Cal/OSHA, 1995) has developed a useful classification system for workplace violence that has been widely adopted.

> **Type I** is *violence by people unrelated to the workplace.* Most fatal workplace violence falls into this category. This includes armed robberies and assaults on workers transporting money and goods. A 1993 U.S. government study showed that 75% of all workplace homicides involved robberies and other crimes against workers in high-risk situations such as retail, taxicab, and armored car services. Police officers and security guards killed in the line of duty accounted for another 10% (Toscano & Weber, 1995).

> **Type II** is *acts committed by people who are related in some way to an employee.* This category accounts for the greatest proportion of serious, nonfatal injury in the workplace. Examples of Type II violence are assaults on health care workers by patients and threats by angry or frustrated clients or customers. Female health care workers, for example, suffer the largest proportion of nonfatal assaults of any employment group, according to U.S. Department of Labor statistics (Barab, 1996a).[1] Recently, employers have begun to pay more attention to domestic and partner violence affecting people at work. This includes not only harassment, stalking, and murder of women while at work by abusive husbands, but also cases of "office obsessions." Chapter 8 takes up this issue in greater detail.

> **Type III** is *violence between employees.* Type III is where we find the "revenge killer." We know from government figures, however, how rare this is: Inter-employee violence accounts for only about 6% of fatalities at work (Barab, 1996a). Most commonly, therefore, Type III violence comes in the form of threats rather than fatalities. We also know, however, that the preponderance of concern about workplace violence is focused on violence between employees. The *perception* that someone from within the workplace may become violent is quite frightening. Why is this fear so compelling?

I believe that inter-employee violence has taken front stage because it touches on the crucial issue of general workplace climate and the effects of stress on employees. When we understand what happens when an employee becomes violent or threatening, or is even *perceived* as dangerous, we will understand some very important things about the relationship of violence to the social and organizational system of the workplace. In fact, using the workplace as a kind of laboratory, we will learn a great deal about violence itself: not only why it happens but how to prevent it.

The Problem With Our Systems

To understand the many forms of violence in the workplace, we must look at the individual as well as the system in which his or her behavior is occurring. Type III workplace violence, in which an employee or former employee acts in a threatening or destructive manner toward fellow employees, superiors, or the property of the workplace, is always the result of the *interaction* between a violence-prone individual and a system that provokes the violence or allows it to happen. Once we understand that violence is the result of this interaction, we will be led directly to concrete methods for preventing its occurrence.[2]

In my 10 years of working with employers on this issue, I have discovered the primary barrier to effective violence prevention: *the tendency to do things the way they have always been done.* Currently, employers use the systems they already have in place when there is a question of threatening behavior or when an act of violence has been committed. These systems include well-established responses to behavioral and performance issues set out by employment law and collective bargaining agreements and procedures to handle worker illness and injury governed by local, state, and federal laws. The legal and bureaucratic origins of these arrangements dictate the form and style of employer-employee relationships around these issues. This style sets employer and employee against one another, and it is this that often sets the stage for a disaster. Consider some prime examples:

- An employee makes a claim that she has been psychologically injured because of an episode at work. In response, the employer engages a psychiatrist to refute the employee's claim of work-related stress and psychological disability. Through this process, an already impaired, stressed, and alienated worker is transformed into an adversary.

- Following federal, state, or provincial statutes, corporate legal departments submit briefs to workers' compensation boards to rule on employees' claims for compensation. Delicate, complex cases of work-based stress or injury are transformed into heartless legalistic exercises.

- Union and company attorneys clash in arbitration hearings to resolve disputes over discipline and terminations. Angry, traumatized, and damaged workers become pawns in political struggles between warring parties.

The scenarios described above are not the aberrations of a few highly flawed systems—these are the normal, time-honored methods for dealing with safety, behavior and health issues at work. They are based—solidly—on rationales grounded in our legal systems. Rules governing union-management dispute resolution are based on mutual mistrust and strict control over information. Policies for dealing with disputes, conflict, and behaviorally impaired employees are written to protect companies from legal liability. Occupational health procedures are designed to contain costs associated with medical care and lost work time. They result in a distancing of the employer from the healing and recovery process (Braverman, 1993). Observe the result: All the while, the employee in question, whose life has already been torn apart by stress, sits forgotten on the sidelines while adversaries clash or bureaucrats move on to the next piece of paper on their desks. The language of law, of government regulations, or of medical diagnoses does not address the truth of the employee's experience. The procedures and approaches dictated by these systems will not resolve the *human* problem that has produced the threat or the fear of violence. As we will see, in some cases these responses actually help create the conditions that breed violence. In many other cases, they play a large part in the failure to detect the real problem and prevent the violence from occurring.

The laws and agreements that govern our employment relationships are based on the same 18th-century concepts that form the roots of modern capitalism (Guillart, 1995, pp. 256-257). These concepts hold that the individual's right to own property is the basis of individual self-esteem and the basis of human freedom and well-being. The relationship between the worker and the employer has been based on this premise: As long as the employee's rights to compensation, privacy, and physical safety are protected, all will be well. We are learning, however, that this does not work. Human beings are not the sum of their property, and physical safety alone does not guarantee a healthy, productive worker. Under the current conditions of constant change and increased demand for productivity, the systems designed to protect employee rights under the letter of the law are breaking down. As the cases to follow will illustrate, they can and do foster deadening isolation and a maddening sense of helplessness and alienation in the healthiest of individuals. In the more vulnerable, they can crush self-esteem and destroy psychological and physical well-being. A prime example happened at a U.S. Postal Service facility.

Thomas McIlvane was the fired postal letter carrier who killed four supervisors and then himself at a Michigan post office in 1991.[3] Over the 8-year period that preceded this act, as McIlvane's threatening behavior escalated, multiple systems protecting his rights and those of his employer and coworkers were activated, including a collective bargaining agreement, federal disability statutes, and laws governing criminal complaints. Mobilized in all of their legalistic and bureaucratic detail, these procedures and systems helped to transform an already unbalanced individual into a desperate man bent on revenge. As we will see in Chapter 4, nothing in the systems designed to protect McIlvane's "rights" allowed the persistent signals of danger to be detected and become the basis for action to confront the rapidly growing threat to his own life and that of others. The delays and lack of coordination between disciplinary, counseling, medical, labor relations, and judicial processes all contributed to his slide into an isolated, desperate, and ultimately fatal condition. Countless other stories from my experience show how established procedures and policies, carried out by well-meaning people doing their jobs, can help drive employees who are already stressed and threatened into violent, threatening, or self-destructive behavior.

To understand why the present approaches are so inadequate and potentially disastrous, we need to understand what causes violent behavior in a workplace context. We will not achieve this understanding by analyzing crime statistics or by studying how to protect our companies from legal liability. We will not learn what we need to know by hearing from psychiatrists or forensic experts who have studied cases of criminal behavior and can analyze the causes and symptoms of violent behavior. *All* of this is useful information, but only when it is applied in a system-level analysis that takes into consideration the complex interaction of individual and social factors. Dr. Robert Fein, a psychologist with the U.S. Secret Service, has studied assassination attempts and other forms of targeted violence. He emphasized the need for improved procedures to guide response to threats:

> Violence is a process, as well as an act. Violent behavior does not occur in a vacuum. Careful analysis of violent incidents shows that violent acts often are the culmination of long-developing, identifiable trails of problems, conflicts, disputes and failures. (Fein et al., 1995, p. 3)

Every employer should understand this basic point and develop policies and procedures accordingly.

The Wages of Stress: What Is Violence?

The assessment of dangerousness in a workplace context involves more than a psychiatric assessment of an individual based on a clinical interview or psychological testing. To understand why this is so, we must understand more about what causes violent behavior. Here is a simple definition: *Violence is the outcome of unbearable stress.* Anyone can become violent when the relevant conditions are provided. Test this for yourself: Think of yourself walking down the street with your toddler, a young niece, or a grandchild in tow. Now imagine that a stranger approaches and tries to snatch the child away. Will you watch passively, or will you act against that person? Think about someone striking or abusing someone you love. Imagine being pushed, day after day, beyond your limit to endure abuse or humiliation by a bully or a person in a position of power. Violence, like most human behaviors, is an attempt to take action in response to a condition, a need, or a demand, and each of us has his or her limit. Having said this, however, we must state the obvious: Under conditions of unbearable stress, some people become violent, and some do not. What, then, are the conditions that allow violence to happen? To understand why a violent act is committed, we have to look at the interaction of three areas: the person, the situation, and the context (Fein et al., 1995).[4] (See Figure 3.1.)

The Person

Unbearable stress can be catastrophic to a person's life. This catastrophe can take many forms, but in general, it will result in one or more of four outcomes: serious or chronic physical illness, emotional breakdown, suicide, or violence.[5] Which personality factors determine that violence will be the outcome? In my experience, the most important have to do with the individual's *interpersonal* functioning—the way in which he sees himself in relationship to other people: What behaviors and styles does he use in his interactions with others?[6] Does he try to understand the other's point of view and to reach mutual agreements, or does he tend to use manipulation and intimidation in his interactions? Is he able to take responsibility for the consequences of his own actions, as opposed to blaming others or "the system" for what goes wrong in his life? Can he feel shame and guilt, or is his sense of right and wrong determined by what he thinks he can "get away with?" Can he control his impulses by anticipating consequences, or does he "act first and think later?" What is the state of his self-esteem? As we will see as we

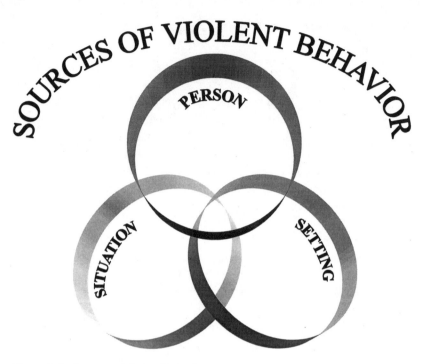

Figure 3.1. Sources of Violent Behavior

continue to explore the causes of violence, the answers to these questions are crucial for an understanding of the potential for violent behavior.

Several other questions must also be asked to assess the risk of violence: What kind of personal and cultural background may have helped shape this person's attitudes about the uses and acceptability of violence? Has the person resorted to violent behavior in the past? If so, under what circumstances?[7] The answers to all of these questions will help us evaluate the person's ability to withstand stress and to find acceptable, useful ways to deal with conflict, anger, frustration, and pressure. On the basis of the answers that we receive, we may assess that this person has the basic skills for dealing with minor and major stressors and that, in the face of life's challenges, he will find ways to be flexible in his thinking, maintain his connections with sources of support, and communicate effectively with others. But if the answers tend in a different direction, we will understand why, over time, he has spiraled ever deeper into the depression and sense of isolation and helplessness that have led finally to violent or self-destructive behavior.

The Situation

Establishing that a person has a predisposition for violence does not yet allow us to make a prediction about violence. The second necessary component is a *situation* that pushes the person toward violent or threatening behavior. In the workplace context, this often has to do with loss, humiliation, and being cut off from other people. Typical examples include loss of employment at mid- or late career, demotion or loss of job security, injury or illness leading to disruption of body image or sense of competence and control, and rejection or threat of abandonment at home (which is often the cause of domestic violence).

These stressors relate directly to the personality issues described in the previous section. When we evaluate a potential for workplace violence, we look in particular for those aspects of the stressor that relate to the individual's connection to interpersonal and organizational supports and those that have an impact on his sense of effectiveness in the world. It is precisely when they feel powerless that some people begin to be at risk for violent or threatening behavior. To understand why this is, we must remember that violence is related to an overwhelming sense of desperation and isolation and a growing sense that nothing the person can do seems to help or change his situation. The type of person described in the section above is someone who is poorly equipped to maintain positive supports when things begin to go wrong. Because he cannot easily understand his own contribution to the problem and instead blames other people or "the system" for his misfortunes, he progressively alienates the people around him and uses up the resources and good will of the systems designed to support him. In these situations, you will often hear managers or coworkers declare, "He's burned us out! There is nothing more we can do for him." This often happens to the union that represents such an employee. Similarly exhausted with the never-ending appeals for help, union stewards or officers will ultimately limit themselves to the minimum responses required by the labor agreement. This causes the person to feel even more isolated. His feelings of desperation intensify, and his depression deepens. That is why, by far, the most potentially dangerous stressors are those that reduce or remove supports to the individual's physical, financial, and social well-being. This leads us directly to the third circle, the setting.

The Setting

Once you have an individual with a predisposition to violence and a situation that pushes that individual past his ability to cope nonviolently, the stage is set for violence. But these ingredients alone are not enough to produce the violent event itself. For the violence to occur, it must be *allowed* to happen. Here is where we look to the workplace's capacity to recognize the warning signs of stress-related breakdown and to take action that will interrupt or affect the process. As we shall see in each of the cases to follow, achieving this capacity is the basis and goal of violence prevention policies and activities. Violence is the result of a process that unfolds over time. In every story that ends in violence, there are several points where the intervention of the system—or lack thereof—contributed directly to the outcome.

As an employer, you have little control over the first circle: The person you hire may possess characteristics that will be impossible to detect and that exist only as a potential at the time that you hire him (I will take up the issue of preemployment screening in a later chapter). You may or may not have control over the second circle, which may involve a family issue, crime in the community, or illness. Even if the situation is workplace generated—for example, a change in working conditions or a layoff—this may be relatively out of the control of the employer. Effective violence prevention depends on the ability of the social or organizational setting to mediate or moderate the effect of those stressors on the individual. The *potential* for violence will be generated through the interaction of the first and second circles. But it is in the third circle that the employer exercises the most control, and it is here that both his responsibility and his opportunity lie (see Figure 3.1).

Effective violence prevention in the workplace consists of two primary components: early notification and stress reduction. The following diagrams illustrate how the employer can make a difference in the outcome of a possible threat of violence. Figure 3.2 shows how the response of a crisis-prone organization can lead to a violent or self-destructive outcome. Beginning at the left, it lists some of the possible *stressors* that can lead to a violent or self-destructive outcome. Depending on individual factors, an employee subjected to any of these stresses may display one or more of the conditions or behaviors listed in the next box of the figure. These are the *warning signals* available to the employer. Once the warning signs appear, the response of crisis-prone organizations can contribute directly to a tragic or destructive outcome. In such a scenario, the signs of distress in the individual are met by the dysfunctional response of an unprepared organization. The most common among these are avoidance of the disruptive or inappropriate behavior, punishment through standard disciplinary procedures, and a narrow, bureaucratic approach to illness or apparent disability. Through these responses, the seeds of personal and organizational crisis are sown, for example:

A bullying, intimidating employee begins to escalate his verbal attacks on his coworkers. Supervisors continue to avoid confrontation with him until tension on

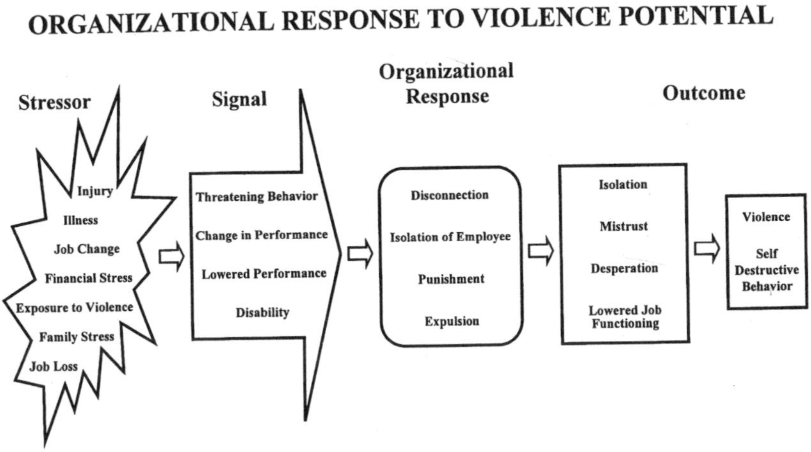

ORGANIZATIONAL RESPONSE TO VIOLENCE POTENTIAL

Figure 3.2. The Effect of Organizational Response on Violence Potential (negative outcome)

the unit erupts into physical violence and severe discipline and possible termination is necessary. This may provoke an even more serious crisis. An employee struggling with depression, marital problems, and a developing cocaine habit is disciplined for poor performance. Aided by his union, he contests this action but soon takes a medical leave because of stress. Inadequately treated for his mental health and chemical dependency problems, he continues to deteriorate. Armed with notes from his family physician, he prolongs his leave indefinitely, fearing a return to the pressure of work. The employer, frustrated by the uncertainty of the employee's status and by the cost of paying a nonproductive worker, finally demands independent assessment of the employee's medical status. A dispute ensues, which ends in a notice of termination. The employee contests, accusing the employer of discrimination. The case goes to arbitration. When he loses, the employee, in a near-suicidal rage, threatens "payback."

These examples show how the crucial point of intervention, in which the early signs of trouble might have been recognized and defused, have instead been missed or mishandled. The at-risk individual moves through increasing distrust, fear, and isolation until he reaches the violent or self-destructive result. As the scenario develops, the organization, showing itself to be crisis prone and having missed the opportunity to change this outcome, moves toward a condition in which reactive crisis management will be the only option.

ORGANIZATIONAL RESPONSE TO VIOLENCE POTENTIAL

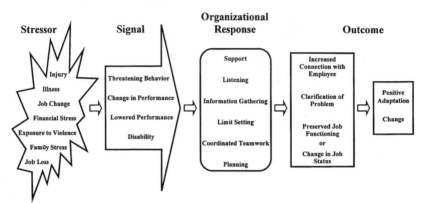

Figure 3.3. The Effect of Organizational Response on Violence Potential (positive outcome)

Figure 3.3 illustrates the alternative, in which the organization's response to the warning signs can make a profound difference. If the employer has established policies that set out clear definitions of unacceptable behavior, he or she will be able to communicate clearly with the employee who is suspected of violating them. Clear limit setting is the foundation of effective communication in these cases. For the employee who is at risk for violence or who is perceived as threatening, this kind of communication is vital because it reduces feelings of helplessness and isolation. Limit setting and clear communication from the employer open a dialogue and produce an alternative to violence. Where once there was isolation and helplessness, there is now a clearly directed alternative arrived at through a process of identification of the unacceptable behavior, information gathering, assessment and analysis, proposing of solutions, and agreement on consequences or necessary changes in the job situation.

Despite the positive tone of the phrases such as "positive adaptation" and "change," the journey to a nonviolent outcome may be far from a "warm and fuzzy" experience for some of the parties. The outcome itself may be separation from the workplace for the offending employee, a painful confrontation with discipline, or the beginnings of a long struggle with mental illness or drug addiction. But it is a *nonviolent* outcome. It replaces the near-certainty of a costly, prolonged ordeal (if not disaster) with the chance of a success. With appropriate and timely intervention, the employer can remedy a long-standing case of mismanagement, identify a poor job placement, or help a troubled employee obtain proper evaluation and treatment.

Summary: Where the Employer Has the Power

In the "setting" circle in Figure 3.1 and the crucial organizational response step in Figure 3.3, the policies and actions of the employer have a direct effect on violence prevention. The "violent employee" can be anyone: You have already hired him, or you may hire him tomorrow. The key is to recognize when the mix of person and situation have created a condition that requires your special attention and to be ready to respond promptly and effectively. The five cases that I will present in the following chapters provide vivid illustrations of this basic principle.

Notes

1. Barab (1996a) provides a comprehensive discussion of the violence risks faced by public and service employees.

2. Mantell (1994, p. 6) offers a 2×2 matrix model. He posits that low levels of employee maturity, interacting with a toxic workplace environment, may produce a high risk of violence.

3. Chapter 4 presents a detailed study of this case.

4. Fein and his colleagues also added a fourth dimension, that of "target," to this risk assessment model. Information about whether a target has been identified, is vulnerable to an attack, and feels afraid of the subject is relevant to the assessment of violence risk.

5. For this formulation and the previous definition of violence as the outcome of unbearable stress, I am grateful to Drs. Robert Fein and John Daignault, who both credit Dr. Shervert Frazier for this simple and powerful formulation.

6. Here, as elsewhere in the book, I use the masculine pronoun when talking about the violent person in general. I do this because, overwhelmingly, perpetrators of violence are male, and I am choosing to avoid the awkward attempt to give "equal time" to both genders when not referring to actual people.

7. The thinking of acknowledged authorities on violence prediction goes against the conventional wisdom that a history of violent behavior is the best and only reliable predictor of violence. John Monahan (1981) looked at how the sociocultural background of the individual might render violence acceptable and under what circumstances. Monahan emphasized the importance of the context of the threat situation, the availability of weapons, the vulnerability of the victim, and the social approval of violence. Fein et al. (1995) reinforced this contextual perspective in their work. Fein's recent research on threats on public figures further casts doubt on the "violent history" hypothesis (see Fein & Vossekuil, 1998).

4

A Post Office Tragedy

We begin to see that all of us are trapped in structures, structures
embedded both in our ways of thinking and in the interpersonal
and social milieus in which we live. Our knee-jerk tendencies to
find fault with one another gradually fade, leaving a much deeper
appreciation of the forces within which we all operate.
Peter Senge, *The Fifth Discipline*

"No, no!" said the Queen. "Sentence first, verdict afterwards!"
Lewis Carroll, *Alice's Adventures in Wonderland*

On November 8, 1991, an arbitrator in Royal Oak, Michigan, signed his ruling on Case C7N-4B-D 29760, *The United States Postal Service vs. the National Association of Letter Carriers.* In it, he upheld the termination of postal letter carrier Thomas McIlvane. Six days later, McIlvane lay mortally wounded on the floor of the post office where he had worked. He had shot and killed four supervisors and then put a bullet into his own head. In carrying out this act, McIlvane made good on a threat he had made repeatedly, in fact over 20 documented times, over a period of years. These threats had grown more specific and more savage during the period after his termination. When news of the Royal Oak tragedy hit the airwaves and print media, workplace violence finally took its place as perhaps the number one preoccupation of the American employer.

"Going Postal": Why the Post Office?

Violence at the U.S. Postal Service has become an emblem for workplace violence in America. Expressions such as "going postal" have become part of our culture. A reference to the post office by an employee in a tense workplace situation is a red flag: It can be compared to saying "I've got a bomb!" while going through airport security. "Postal" references, if the timing and circumstances are right, can be grounds for discipline, or at least for an unpleasant conversation with the boss or a specialist hired to assess whether you are a danger to your fellow workers. Why is this so? What, if any, is the basis for this reputation? Let us start by clearing up a couple of myths.

Myth 1: Postal workers as a group are more violent than other people. This is not true. In fact, in my over 10 years of experience working with the Postal Service, I found postal workers, as a group, to be among the most patient and self-controlled people I have ever met.[1] It is sad and unfair that these three-quarters of a million good, hard-working Americans have had to bear this stigma and tolerate the constant barrage of tasteless "postal" humor.

Myth 2: Abusive postal managers drive workers to violence and sometimes even to murder. This patently simplistic analysis is inaccurate in specifics as well as in principle. There are, of course, incidents of abusive management in the Postal Service. But abusive managers do not create or provoke homicidal violence. A potentially homicidal individual requires more than a good excuse or a likely target to commit murder—it just isn't that simple.[2]

This is one of the most important lessons to be learned from the Royal Oak shootings: If you settle for simple explanations and easy targets of blame, you are doomed to perpetuate the conditions that gave rise to the tragedy. The problem at Royal Oak was not primarily the people—it was the system.

As we discussed in the last chapter, human behavior can be understood only in the context in which it occurs. Violence results when qualities in the individual, the specific situation, and the overall organizational and social system converge. Thomas McIlvane was violent in the extreme—and he showed himself to be dangerous in many ways and over a long period of time. At any of many points in the development of this story, his violence should have been detected and action taken to assess the risk and respond appropriately. This was the job of the system, and the system failed. The Postal Service did not create Tom McIlvane; the sad fact is that in the early stages of this story, he looked much like the thousands of intimidating, scary, or unbalanced people who threaten others in American work-places every day. But by the end of the story, he lay dead along with his victims. His personality and the system that hired him were a deadly mix. He should have been stopped, and very likely could have been stopped. So this story is not about him. It is about a system that failed.

A Crisis-Prone Environment

The Postal Service that hired Thomas McIlvane in the early 1980s was equipped with multiple systems designed to protect health and well-being on the job. As a Postal Service employee, McIlvane enjoyed all the benefits available to the modern employee: full health and disability coverage, guarantee of treatment for job-related injury and illness, and the right to sick time and to a humane work schedule. If these guarantees should falter, there was a union and a collective bargaining agreement to direct the resolution of disputes in a fair manner. Federal statutes provided yet another set of protections from unfair or discriminatory management practices. Finally, the Postal Service had its own internal security and law enforcement body, the Postal Inspection Service. Its mission was to protect the Postal Service from crime, both from outside and from postal employees.

In fact and practice, however, the system often worked against these very goals and principles. Postal work is complex, demanding, and stressful. It is highly time driven: There are always huge volumes of mail that must be sorted and delivered. Work demands are subject to constantly changing conditions, including mail volume, weather, and equipment breakdown. Given these facts, there are few industries as much in need of flexible management and work design practices, communication and collaboration between workers and management, and atten-tion to warning signs of stress in individuals and work groups.

Unfortunately, postal employees in the 1980s and early 1990s still worked under one of the most rigid and adversarial systems in American industry. Long-standing mistrust between management and labor, and even among the four unions themselves, hampered managers' ability to apply creative or flexible solutions to production or service problems. Chronically poor communication forced parties to rely on the cumbersome and adversarial grievance-arbitration system for the resolution of even the most trivial disputes or disagreements. Managers and bargaining unit employees alike felt isolated and beleaguered when they found themselves in stressful situations, whether these arose from work or nonwork situations. Workers in need of accommodation in work hours or job demands confronted a system that was more interested in maintaining the rules than in preserving the well-being of the individual employee. Employees who were injured, sick, or breaking down under stress faced a disability and occupational health care system that was heartbreakingly bureaucratic, based more on protecting against fraud than on returning employees to work whole and healthy. Employees who were physically or mentally impaired therefore confronted a system that distanced them from the employer, removed them from sources of support, and made them feel frustrated and mistrusted rather than valued.

In the fall of 1991, these conditions had taken their toll on overall workplace morale and on the occupational and individual health of postal employees in management and union alike. Costs associated with sick time, absenteeism, and workers' compensation claims and the mammoth legal and administrative costs of unending grievance and arbitration activity compared in magnitude only with the human costs of living in an environment where mistrust and conflict were the rule. Although a horrific mass murder in a Postal Service facility in Edmund, Oklahoma, by a letter carrier in the late 1980s (De Becker, 1997, pp. 143-144) had raised questions about workplace climate and labor relations, many postal facilities and divisions still struggled with the task of meeting challenging service demands in the context of a basically adversarial and unhealthy work environment. This was the stage on which the Royal Oak tragedy unfolded.

The Shootings at Royal Oak

At 8:45 a.m. on November 14, 1991, Thomas McIlvane, armed with a loaded semiautomatic rifle, entered the main post office in Royal Oak, Michigan, through an unsecured rear loading dock. He strode purposefully through the building, climbing the stairs to the supervisors' offices on the second floor. Seeking out particular supervisors and managers who had been involved with his discipline and ultimate termination, McIlvane discharged over 100 rounds from his weapon, shooting eight people and killing or mortally wounding four before taking his own life. The shootings took place against the backdrop of extremely poor labor relations in the Royal Oak division, allegations of questionable management practices, operational and service problems, and recent management changes.

The Person: Who Was Thomas McIlvane?

The official record tells us very little about McIlvane's background. The congressional investigation turned up nothing besides a tour of duty with the U.S. Marine Corps. His military career was characterized by insubordination, use of foul, aggressive language to superiors, and overtly violent acts against people and equipment, for which he was disciplined repeatedly, including being sentenced to a 3-month incarceration. Ultimately, he was discharged, under the confusing and sanitized military category of "General Under Honorable Conditions." In fact, McIlvane had been a highly problematic enlistee who showed clearly violent and antisocial tendencies. None of this, however, was evident from the military discharge record available to the Postal Service at the time of his hiring. Although the question of military records is a special case, this is an issue faced by most employers: the unavailability or unreliability of information from former employers. When this problem is added to the strict limits imposed under the Americans with Disabilities Act on what information can be used to reject an applicant for employment, "screening out" potentially violent individuals becomes more difficult as a prevention strategy. In terms of Royal Oak, however, the issue of McIlvane's prepostal record is interesting but ultimately beside the point. The most important information for an understanding of this tragedy is the postal record itself.

History of Discipline and Health Referrals

McIlvane was hired as a letter carrier in January 1985. In early 1988, the record shows repeated and escalating conflicts with authority, insubordinate, rebellious behavior, and the frequent use of profanity when dealing with superiors. Between October 1988 and August 8, 1990, the date he was issued a notice of removal from the Postal Service, approximately nine incidents of behavioral and performance violations are recorded, which were responded to by a range of disciplinary and investigative procedures. These violations included an alleged assault on a postal customer, which resulted in an Inspection Service investigation; safety violations involving his vehicle, which resulted in a 14-day suspension; throwing a pencil at a supervisor during an argument; and hurling a string of profanity and threats at a female supervisor during a telephone conversation. Besides the disciplinary record, two medical or mental health contacts are documented. In June 1988, McIlvane was sent to the Employee Assistance Program (EAP) because of drug and alcohol abuse. This was followed by a visit to a physician (nonpsychiatrist), who noted "no history of emotional disorders" and found him free of emotional instability and not in need of a psychiatric consultation.

Removal Process

On August 8, 1990, a Removal Notice was issued to McIlvane regarding "profane threats and insubordination" against three supervisors during telephone conversations. Over the next 14 months, the grievance procedure went through the prescribed steps of denial and resubmission on its way to arbitration. The arbitration, which finally took place on October 29, 1991, upheld McIlvane's removal. The arbitrator's decision and award was dated November 8, 1991, *fully 15 months after the Removal Notice had been issued.*

Threats

The congressional investigation that followed the shootings documented over 20 threats that were made by McIlvane toward postal supervisors during the period between his removal and the denial of his grievance. Several examples will illustrate this. On September 20th, McIlvane called his former manager, saying, "You are the one who got me fired. . . . I'm going to be watching you and I'm going to get you." At an unemployment compensation hearing several days later, McIlvane said to a supervisor, "You might win today, but I'm going to get you." In November, McIlvane visited the post office to file again for unemployment benefits. Before leaving, he crumpled the application and threw it in the face of one of the office staff. He then called the manager, saying, "I'm going to come up there and kill you." Numerous attempts of several managers to obtain restraining orders through local law enforcement and to obtain protection from the Inspection Service yielded inconsistent responses and conflicting pieces of advice and ultimately were without result.

The abusive and threatening phone calls continued throughout the following year, coming to the attention of both management and union, at the same time that labor relations activity involving steps in the grievance process were pursued. Union and management did not discuss the threats, except for one instance when the shop steward who worked with McIlvane told a supervisor that McIlvane had a "list" of five supervisors whom he was "going to get." During the congressional investigation, the Letter Carriers Union vice president told an investigator that he was personally aware of threats but felt that it would have been a violation of his legal responsibility to the union member to discuss them with the Postal Service.

On November 8, 1991, the arbitration was concluded with McIlvane's termination upheld. He was notified by telephone through a message left on an answering machine. Three days later, McIlvane went to the post office to carry out his retaliatory threat.

The People: Who Was to Blame?

There are no villains in this piece. Everyone involved, from management, the union, law enforcement, and the judicial system, was doing his or her best to do the job that had been assigned by the system. In confronting this crisis, each was handicapped by his or her experience with a system that had reinforced obedience to the rules and discouraged consultation or creative problem solving. In effect, all the players obeyed a set of unwritten rules that did not allow them to communicate with one another or to seek solutions to a situation that was rapidly spinning out of control. Union officials would have been conditioned to see McIlvane's behavior as yet another response to abusive management practices. Even if they were worried by the reports of McIlvane's actions and threats, they would have felt that they had to advocate for him out of pure opposition to management. Postal human resources, for its part, operated out of the same rigid adherence to narrow roles: This was a standard situation of "hardball" discipline, to be followed by a process of negotiation and deal making about the ultimate severity of punishment. Line and middle managers, bystanders to this essentially political process, who had seen problem employees like this one returned to their charge again and again, angrier and bolder than before, reacted with bitterness and ultimately with helplessness and resignation. Feeling abandoned by their leadership, they would be the last to raise the level of concern to an appropriate organizational level.

The Postal Inspection Service, which was to be criticized soundly in the subsequent congressional report, responded inconsistently to requests for help from management. Already stretched beyond its ability to respond to every request for help from managers, and hampered by having to carry on its investigative activities often in total lack of coordination with management and local law enforcement, the Inspection Service was chronically in a position of having to ration its responses to requests for help. In addition, postal managers were constantly calling on inspectors to respond to behavioral emergencies and to essentially make quick judgments on the severity of a situation. Typically, these situations involved conflicts between unionized employees and supervisors. It was a classic—and tragic—"cry wolf" scenario.

The postal medical department, external physicians, and external judicial and law enforcement personnel fell into the same trap. Hampered by a system that had no mechanisms by which a situation could be identified as a crisis and no procedures for a coordinated response to a health or safety crisis, as well as by inconsistent (or nonexistent) messages about the urgency of this particular situation, the data-gathering and intervention activities of these players were rendered completely ineffective. EAP counselors providing counseling, physicians performing fitness for duty evaluations, judges, and local police all did their own jobs without the benefit of information from or consultation with one another.

And what about the arbitrator? After stating his reasons for denying the grievance, the arbitrator summed up his opinion by duly citing the article and section of the collective bargaining agreement as support for the justice of the removal:

> By his own actions, the grievant has rendered himself unfit for continued employment. Efforts to rehabilitate him through progressive discipline and counseling failed prior to his discharge, and just cause existed under Article 3B and Article 16, #1, for his removal as an employee of the Postal Service. (*United States Postal Service vs. the National Association of Letter Carriers,* 1991)

Having thus stated the reasons for his decision, the arbitrator closed his written statement with the following interesting statement: "His conduct following the discharge certainly will not allow this arbitrator to return him to employment." We know what conduct the arbitrator is referring to in this statement, although these are not issues that are taken up in the opinion that preceded it, which appropriately limits itself to his behavior prior to termination. He is referring to the threats that were made by McIlvane *after his dismissal,* threats about what he would do if he lost the arbitration. The arbitrator, therefore, is making it clear that he knew about the threats, even to the extent of considering them as part of his decision to uphold the termination. He thus must be added to the list of people who were *clearly aware* that a threat existed and who were unable to take any effective action in concert with others who knew. Did the arbitrator consider having a conversation with the representative of the Postal Service or of the union—both of whom had attended the arbitration sessions—about the clear and present danger that existed? Did he wonder if he were mandated by statute or precedent to warn possible victims of a threat to them? Did he wonder if he was himself a potential target of this man?

Like the other players in this drama, the arbitrator should not be faulted for his failure to do any of these things. Like them, he may have been concerned about the danger and even frightened for his own safety. Like them, however, the arbitrator was accustomed to staying inside the confines of the role that had been defined for him by the system. This system, based on settling battles between adversaries, does not allow for communication, consultation, and management of these kinds of crises. As a rule-based, adversarial framework, it functions to distance the people involved from their most basic sense of fear and even their common sense.[3] Our arbitrator, like the union president, the company lawyer, the medical director, and the human resources manager, was trapped in this system. It would be easy to distance ourselves from them, saying, "I would never have been so foolish or blind." Rather than casting stones, however, we should be identifying with their situation. By using their example to examine this issue, we owe it to them to draw lessons from their experience and to ask the question: Does this have to be?

How Could Royal Oak Have Been Different?

What if the events leading up to the Royal Oak murders had been handled differently? To answer this question, let us imagine that the events described here had occurred in a postal district in 1994. As a result of a joint labor-management initiative in the wake of the events of the early 1990s, this postal district, like many others, now had in place a violence prevention plan that was supported by well-established and well-communicated policies and was administered by a trained team of management and bargaining unit staff operating with the full support of their leadership. This very different reality would produce a markedly different result at any level of threat: early or late, mild or acute.

Initial Response to Threats

The first time Thomas McIlvane behaved or spoke in a threatening way, a team composed of representatives from management and labor would be informed of the incident. The team would have designated members from labor and management to talk to McIlvane about the threat that he was alleged to have made. McIlvane would be informed that if he had truly threatened anyone, or had even behaved to create a threatening or violent atmosphere, he was in violation of the policy against workplace violence. He would be told that he might be subject to discipline but that the first order of business was to fully investigate the alleged threat. The investigation, he would be told, might include interviews with people who were involved or who might have information. If it was determined that a real concern existed, he would be requested to meet with a threat assessment specialist. The results of that assessment would be shared with the team and with McIlvane himself. When all the information was collected, the team would reach a decision. Until that time, he would be removed from the workplace and placed on administrative leave with pay. Effectively, any discipline would be deferred.

This scenario presents a radical departure from the traditional *modus operandi* of the Postal Service. Two processes that were once totally separated from and uncoordinated with one another—discipline and medical/psychological assessment—have been replaced by a single, integrated process of comprehensive information gathering. Thus, if McIlvane had made his first threats in 1994, fact finding and decision making on all fronts would have been conducted in a manner that was open and transparent to all, including McIlvane himself.

Prompt Administrative Action

In this scenario, it is unlikely that McIlvane would have ever returned to the workplace, for a comprehensive investigation of his work history, including his military record, combined with a competent mental health assessment would have indicated how impaired and potentially out of control he was. Had he been returned to work, it would have been with clear conditions about the consequences of future threatening behavior. Separating McIlvane earlier in his postal career would have greatly reduced the risk of retaliatory violence by setting a clear limit early in the process. McIlvane would have learned immediately and unequivocally that this behavior would not be tolerated. In the actual scenario, his threatening and inappropriate behavior was actually reinforced through the employer's ineffective response over a period of years. In effect, McIlvane *learned* that he could act this way as a postal employee. When the separation finally came, he felt enraged and betrayed.

Coordinated Response to Emergent Threat

What if reports indicated that threats were escalating and that an acutely dangerous situation existed? In this case, the team would again go into action, feeding all available information into a centrally coordinated process involving internal security and local law enforcement. Possible actions would include warning and protection of potential victims, surveillance of the suspected perpetrator, restraining orders or arrest warrants, and increased security for facilities. All those with information or a possible role in the response would be contacted and would be fully informed and aware of their responsibilities in the situation. In particular, there would be no question of constraints on communication on the part of health providers, union officials, or attorneys. All the players would be aware of their responsibility to protect against this kind of danger. This would apply similarly to an arbitrator or other neutral who might be involved in the current crisis or might have had significant involvement in the past.

The Postal Service Moves Toward the Future

The shootings at Royal Oak were a pivotal, shaping event for the Postal Service. The event dramatically thrust the agency into the public eye. It instantly created two images of the Service. The first was that of the "disgruntled postal worker." This is the image that has established itself in the popular culture and that promotes the endless questions about why postal workers are "so violent." The image is of a man on the edge: angry, stressed to the breaking point, ready to react with murderous violence against the nearest victim if pushed any further. The second image is that of an abusive, sadistic, out-of-control system—authoritarian, cruel, and totally out of step with the times. Workers, oppressed, desperate, and trapped, react with resentment, poor service, sullen, threatening attitudes toward the public, and periodic eruptions of violence.

Federal Efforts

However unfair or inaccurate these images, their proliferation throughout our society has hit the Postal Service hard. The experience has motivated an enormous effort of self-examination and self-correction. Since the Royal Oak tragedy, the Postal Service has devoted a great deal of its energy to attempting to "correct" this presumed problem of violence. At the federal level, the agency has approached this fix in several ways. Public relations events have cast the Postmaster General as a crusader for corporate reform through public events about violence prevention. The Postal Inspection Service has been charged with improving internal information and early response systems to possible threats of violence. Internal "hotlines" have been established to promote early alerts and ease stress. Hiring practices have been investigated and critiqued. Committees have developed systems to detect and correct "hot spots" of employee discontent and management dysfunction, and teams to intervene. Some of these plans have more merit than others. Some have been thwarted or handicapped by the sheer size and bureaucratic unwieldiness of the Service and by the highly political nature of relations between the unions and management at the federal level. The support from the federal level, however, has led to important initiatives at the local level.[4]

Local Efforts

In the years since Royal Oak, efforts at the local level have produced excellent results in a number of postal districts (a district is an administrative unit covering a state or metropolitan area, typically including 6,000 to 10,000 employees). In these districts, responding to the initiative of talented and visionary managers, equally courageous labor leaders have joined with management and the Inspection Service to form active and collaborative violence prevention teams. Developing their own policies and team procedures, they have trained themselves, supervisors, and rank and file in the causes of violence and in alternative methods of responding to these situations. In this way, they have begun to produce genuine change in the culture of mistrust, isolation, and helplessness that helped produce the Royal Oak tragedy.

Conclusion: The Mailman as Everyman

Why has our collective imagination been so captured by the frightening picture of the friendly, daily visitor to our neighborhoods turned into a homicidal monster? Could the image of the disgruntled mailman be a projection of what so many of us feel about the dehumanizing effect of work on our psyches and on our sense of ourselves? Do we perhaps feel that we have lost control of the systems that govern work and that we are in danger of losing sight of our culture's values of freedom of expression, dignity, and self-determination? If this is true, it applies equally to the assembly line worker as to the hard-driving executive climbing the corporate ladder. The efforts of the Postal Service to learn from its painful experience provide a powerful lesson for our entire culture of work and society. The case histories to follow will provide further explorations into these questions.

Notes

1. A 1994 research report from the U.S. Department of Health and Human Services attempted to address this question by comparing national workplace homicide rates with Postal Service homicide rates for the period between 1983 and 1989. Although these data are somewhat hard to interpret, the authors concluded that the rate of homicide in the Postal Service is actually lower than that of the general U.S. working population. De Becker (1997) also debunked the myth that postal employees are more violent.

2. Vern K. Baxter (1994) attempted, in his own words, to "forge a theoretical link" between violence and an organizational climate that creates a sense of personal degradation and frustration. In so doing, he committed what I call the Postal Fallacy because he failed to establish an actual link between the climate at the post office and the cases of postal violence. Baxter committed the same causal fallacies as the sources he quoted to support his theory: namely, postal union spokespersons and some psychologists who had worked with postal employees in the aftermath of several of the murders. The unions would like to believe that management abuses cause the murders and to have others believe that as well. The psychologists, concerned with the emotional health of survivors, and disposed to adopt an empathic stance vis-à-vis individuals who are clearly suffering from having to work in a highly stressful environment, also tend to support a simple causal perspective. The problem is that these untested assumptions encourage one-dimensional solutions, such as changes in management practices or attempts to identify "potentially violent" employees.

3. For a powerful discussion of this issue, see De Becker (1997).

4. Senge (1990), among other modern management theorists, emphasized the importance of actions at the local level. The ability of units at the local level to produce innovative, flexible, and effective programs is well known. The role of the central level should be to support, not dictate, the development of preventive and health-promoting programs.

5

A Modern Witch Hunt

He who believes in the Devil, already belongs to him.
Thomas Mann, *Doctor Faustus*

The cure can be worse than the disease.
Peter Senge, *The Fifth Discipline*

Four hundred years ago in the village of Salem, Massachusetts, 19 people, most of them women, were tried and put to death for being "witches." The term *witch hunt* describes the scapegoating of social deviants and other objects of fear throughout the ages. Sadly, it now has visited the modern American workplace, where the term has begun to make an appearance in reference to the fear of violent employees menacing coworkers in the workplace. *Witch hunt* aptly describes what can happen in the crucibles of conflict, fear, and stress that many of our workplaces have become. In this chapter, we will look at what can happen when three conditions intersect: a downsizing, a crisis-prone organizational culture, and an employee perceived as deviant.

Our Modern Witch Hunts

To understand how witch hunts can happen in the workplace, we need only pay a visit to a company in the throes of a downsizing. As we arrive on the scene, the first thing we notice is what has happened to trust between people. No one believes what anyone says anymore. As layoffs and restructuring proceed, anxiety and skepticism reign. As information about the future becomes a preoccupation, leaders, almost always acting in good faith, make promises and assurances about the future. "No more cuts!" they will proclaim, and they believe it, desperately reassuring their employees as well as themselves that the job losses will be limited and will end. Experience has proven that this is rarely the case. Change proceeds relentlessly. Promises about job security are invariably broken. Because of what happens to information, people begin to mistrust the veracity and credibility of leadership. The boss, who at one time may have been seen as benevolent, fair, honest, and straightforward, is now perceived as unscrupulous, unfeeling, and a liar. Where before an atmosphere of teamwork, security, and safety prevailed, there is an uneasy sense of fear, rage, and resentment. Who will be the next to go? Who can you believe?

In this atmosphere, tolerance for diversity breaks down. Behavior that may have been accepted in the past now takes on a sinister, threatening cast. In our modern scenario, the embodiment of this fear is the image of the angry, homicidal worker who acts out the rage against the institution. People who do not fit the mold of an average worker suddenly become the objects of this fear. Who, people wonder, will act out the rage that everyone is feeling, if not the "loner," the bully, the outspoken, "masculine" woman, the Vietnam veteran, the manic depressive?

Echoes of the Past

The parallels to the witch trials 400 years ago hold interesting lessons for us. In seeking explanations for this frightening episode in our history, writers about the witch trials have offered a number of interpretations, ranging from fear of women to economic greed. The most intelligent analyses of the events that took place in Salem, Massachusetts in 1692, however, view this paroxysm of fear and its murderous consequences in the context of the social and political events of that particular time and place (Hansen, 1969; Karlsen, 1987). Salem village of the late 17th century was a place of seething conflicts and deep animosities over political power and divergent economic interests. Prosperous townspeople and poor farmers alike were beset by intense fears brought on by the fast-paced economic and social changes occurring at the time. Uncertainty reigned about who would maintain power over the means of production and the social infrastructure of a society rapidly outgrowing the rigid moral and political strictures of the original Puritan settlers. The fear and mistrust between these factions threatened to reach levels of violence—if not in deed, certainly in word. It was this condition of social disruption and uncertainty that set off the short-lived but highly destructive hysteria of the witch trials.

Can this historical parallel help us understand our society's intense interest in workplace violence and the preoccupation with the "revenge" perpetrator? As has been noted repeatedly in this book, times of change and turmoil challenge existing societal and organizational structures and create the need for innovative, courageous solutions. Colonial Americans lived in an environment of rapid change and unremitting insecurity. In the centers of power, men searched for ways to meet the challenges of the new realities. They struggled to make existing forms of governance and methods of law and jurisprudence meet the intense, immediate needs of a society in crisis. Without the benefit of experience, and in an environment of uncertain and shifting leadership, these methods often faltered. This is what happened in Salem Village, and this is precisely where we find ourselves as we analyze the issue of workplace violence in America today. As new systems are being tested, established modes of power, decision making, and values are being challenged. Mistakes are being made, often with serious consequences. The present case is an example of just that.

Salem, 1993: The Case of Northern Digital[1]

Northern Digital had been burned once. Early in 1990, an employee for this company of about 3,000 employees, which manufactures communications equipment and provides customer service for an eight-state area, had carried out a fatal threat against a coworker. Although the act was not committed at the workplace, senior management was spurred to develop a violence prevention program. A policy was written, consultants were hired to provide training materials, and a group of appropriate people from security, human resources, and health and safety were designated as the team responsible for the program. On paper, it looked fine. However, the project stalled. The policy was never publicized. The "team" never met to be trained or make decisions about how it would function in the event of a threat or an act of violence. Despite its efforts, therefore, the company was unprepared when, one day in 1993, three employees reported a possible threat situation. This was a disaster in which no shots were fired, and no hand was even raised in anger, but it was a disaster nevertheless. This story is a saddening example of how well-meaning company personnel permanently damaged an employee and ended her career when they attempted to respond to a report that she made a threat against a supervisor. We will see how the company was drawn into a costly legal battle, a battle that involved loyal and hard-working employees in a demoralizing, frustrating, and painful effort to defend the company's destructive and highly flawed actions against a single individual.

Act I: The Alarm

In the spring of 1993, Northern Digital was an industry suffering the agony of deregulation. Having been protected from competition for years, it now had to trim its staff and reorganize its operations to survive. This process had been ongoing for about 18 months, and employees, having lived through a series of cuts at several organizational levels, were frightened, demoralized, and angry. Line and middle managers, their ranks thinned through a series of layoffs, felt mistrustful of the company and out of touch with their superiors. At the same time, they felt mistrusted and resented by the employees who reported to them. Interpersonal tension, fear, and mistrust were at high levels in most departments.

Pam Norcross had worked for Northern Digital for 23 years. Divorced, in her late 40s, and an energetic, outgoing woman, Pam had advanced from an entry-level job to a line management position. Pam was, in her own words, "colorful." She was well known throughout her department for her direct, outspoken ways. Even her friends described her as occasionally crude and even abrasive. Her speech was often peppered with sexual and violent metaphors. It was, she would claim at the arbitration, the way she had behaved for her entire quarter-century tenure at the company. One day in that spring of 1993, during a conversation about one of the managers who had presided over many of the cuts and had become the focus of resentment and unhappiness, three women who worked with Pam overheard her remark that she would "blow away" this particular manager if he "got in her face." Increasingly anxious about the growing tension in the work environment, and having just seen a television program about workplace violence, these women felt it was important to report this information to company management. They went to George Kramer, who headed the department, and reported Pam's statement to him.

Act II: The Response

George, distressed at what he heard, decided to take the report seriously. However, he was at a loss about what to do. He was vaguely aware that there was a company policy that was supposed to cover such things, but he had never received any training or information about it. He called the medical director for advice. The medical director was not available, so he talked to Helen, a social worker who worked in the medical department. After hearing George's report of an employee threatening to kill her boss, Helen informed George that the employee would have to undergo a psychological assessment and that she would arrange this with the external provider who was contracted to perform mental health services for the company. Helen was also unaware of any special policy governing threats. Her advice to George was based on her understanding of the standard company policy for a "fitness-for-duty" evaluation. This evaluation was called into service when a behavioral or physical condition interfered with job functioning. Following Helen's direction, George decided that the next action would be to have Pam's immediate supervisor meet with her to inform her of the requirement to undergo this evaluation. Neither George nor Helen was aware that in so doing, they were both already in violation of key components of the company's fitness-for-duty procedures.

The next day, following George's request, Pam's supervisor Cathy, who was also Pam's friend, asked Pam out to lunch, where she informed her that certain "unnamed coworkers" had come to management about statements that Pam had made about shooting the boss. Cathy informed Pam that because of this report, she was to submit to a psychological evaluation to determine if she posed a threat. At this time, Cathy also told Pam that she thought that the charges were "ridiculous" but that she hoped that Pam would cooperate. Pam agreed to go. Unaware, as were George and Helen, of the requirement to inform Pam that the interview would not be confidential and that all information might be turned over to the employer, Cathy did not tell Pam that she would be required to sign a release of information.

Act III: The Investigation:
Crossed Signals, Fumbled Communications

The following day, Pam arrived at the offices of Moreland Associates Inc., a psychological treatment and consultation group. A receptionist handed her a stack of forms to complete. They included a four-page personal and medical history data questionnaire and a legal form authorizing release of all information to her employer. Unprepared for this, Pam was upset and nervous about providing this information and releasing it to her employer. She refused to complete or sign the forms. The interview proceeded anyway. There is some dispute about whether the social worker at Moreland Associates agreed to inform Pam about the results of the evaluation, but the fact remains that no one called Pam, either from the psychologist's office or from the company, to inform her of the results of the evaluation. Simply, no one had been designated to do so. In the meantime, the company knew nothing because the clinician did not report any results to the company, only that Pam had refused to sign the releases.

When Pam reported to work the following day, she was summoned to the security office, where she met with a security manager and her third- and fourth-level supervisors. At that time, Pam was confronted with the charges that she had threatened a supervisor. Pam protested that her statements were made in jest, that she did not intend to hurt anyone, and that, further, she had made such statements in the past and was not aware of any policy that prohibited such statements. Pam was then informed that she was suspended for refusing to complete the forms at the psychologist's office. She immediately agreed to complete the requested documents and to return to the psychologist to complete a standard psychological test, the Minnesota Multiphasic Personality Inventory (MMPI). Pam returned to the psychologist and completed the MMPI. She was told that she would be informed of the results. Confused and highly anxious, Pam waited to be informed of the results and about her expected return to work. By the following Monday, she had not heard from anyone. By then, she was experiencing crying spells and loss of appetite. On Monday afternoon, she called the psychologist's office and was informed that the results of the MMPI were "satisfactory."

Act IV: The Decision

Meanwhile, the managers were attempting to assemble information and reach a decision. Cathy, Pam's supervisor, had a brief conversation with the psychologist from Moreland who had met with Pam. Although a written report would not be forthcoming for weeks, and although the psychologist was unaware that Pam had now signed the releases, she told Cathy that there was no evidence that Pam presented a danger to the workplace. Cathy made no attempt to communicate this to George or any other manager. No one from the company had yet contacted Pam.

George met with Marian, the security manager, and Cathy to discuss what to do. At that time, they had not been in touch with Helen from health services, except for the earlier communication about Pam's failure to complete the forms. George's notes from this meeting, as recorded in his deposition months later, read: "We still do not have a report on the threat of violence from the evaluation." Marian reported a number of facts about Pam based on hearsay and rumor from her conversations with several employees. These related to her emotionality, her instability in the aftermath of cancer surgery, and reports that she owned a knife that she talked about taking to work with her. George, Cathy, and Marian believed, in the absence of any information to the contrary, that Pam was possibly mentally unbalanced and that they and other employees had reason to take her threats seriously. On the basis of these assumptions, they came to a decision. George phoned Pam, requesting her to report for a meeting the next day.

Pam met with George and the others as requested. She was suspended for 3 weeks without pay "due to the seriousness of her statements." To return to work at the conclusion of the suspension, Pam would be required to attend a class on how to get along with others. George justified the suspension on the basis of the company's violence-in-the-workplace policy, although he acknowledged to Pam that the policy had never been communicated to her or to other employees. He told her that she would receive a letter concerning the suspension and the required training. However, on the advice of the company's lawyers, this letter was not written. Pam went home to wait for the letter that never came. Her emotional condition deteriorated rapidly, with dramatic weight loss, uncontrolled crying, and severe depression. She entered treatment with a psychotherapist.

Two weeks after Pam was suspended, her primary care physician wrote to the company that because of the extreme stress reaction she was experiencing, he would not release Pam to return to work. Unable to work, Pam filed a claim for disability based on her emotional condition. The company, meanwhile, had received the psychologist's original report, which stated that Pam did not present a danger to others and was psychologically normal and able to work. On the basis of this, the company required that Pam return to the psychologist for a second evaluation to determine whether she qualified for medical benefits! In response to this request, Pam's physician wrote a letter to Northern Digital stating that she was totally disabled and that she "might never recover from the emotional trauma she has experienced." The company sent Pam a letter offering her the option of retirement. After a confusing exchange of paperwork, the company finally changed the offer to disability retirement, which would provide more generous benefits. It would be fully one year, however, before the retirement was granted.

Act V: The Lawsuit

Six months later, in treatment for severe depression, barely able to leave her home, and unable to work, Pam Norcross initiated a lawsuit against Northern Digital. The suit enumerated 11 claims for relief, including harassment and discrimination for a perceived disability (e.g., emotional instability, dangerousness), negligence in training its supervisors and security personnel in responding to and investigating possible threats, and negligence in the supervision of company personnel in the requiring and administration of psychological testing. The suit also cited the company's failure to disclose its violence policy to Pam and other employees and closed by claiming that "defendant breached its fiduciary duty to plaintiff as a longterm employee to understand her personality, interview fully her coworkers and supervisors, treat her with the respect she deserved, and maintain her dignity as a hard-working, loyal twenty-four year employee." The case was taken before an arbitrator. After 10 days of hearings, the case was decided in favor of the company. The arbitrator decided that Pam Norcross had failed to show that the company had broken any laws governing discrimination against employees.

Lessons Learned

The name "Northern Digital" is fictitious, as are the names of the people introduced in these pages, but this is the story of a real company. I was the expert hired by "Pam Norcross" and her lawyer to help her pursue the case against her former employer. I spent many hours during the arbitration hearing looking across the room at "George Kramer," the manager who had presided over Pam's ordeal. As a middle manager and good corporate soldier, he continued to serve his time in what had become the purgatory of this case by representing the company at the arbitration. As the hearing continued, I saw the look in his eyes and the grim set of his shoulders that expressed the pain that he carried from the entire affair. Near the end of the hearings, in response to a question from Norcross's lawyer, Kramer said that if he had known then what he knew now, he never would have proceeded against Norcross in the way he did. At the next break, Pam Norcross crossed the room, took George Kramer by the hand, and thanked him for saying what he did. Kramer, tears in his eyes, embraced Norcross, and said to her, "I never meant to hurt you." Later, Pam told us that for her, the case was over at that point. This acknowledgment was what she needed, more than any legal resolution.

This moment illustrates powerfully the extent of the company's real losses in this case. Kramer and the other managers and functionaries who had been dragged through this affair knew clearly by the end how tragically their roles had played out. The top executives, who remained invisible throughout the affair, had, unknowingly, lost the loyalty and confidence of these managers and, ultimately, of every other Northern Digital employee who had witnessed the unfolding and ultimate resolution of this episode. Recent research on job loss (Skarlicki, Ellard, & Kelln, 1998) supports the notion that how a company *carries out* a decision is more important than its actual consequences. The "procedural justice effect" holds that people's perceptions of the fairness of a decision are based on how they perceive it was carried out, not on the actual outcome of the decision. Research has shown that attitudes about the fairness of a layoff depend on whether the victims of the layoffs have a voice in the process and how sensitively the company communicates about what is happening. "It wasn't what they ended up doing that was devastating to me," I have heard countless laid-off and fired employees say, "It's how they did it!" We know also that the survivors of layoffs suffer serious negative effects on their health, morale, and productivity when company leadership does not handle the layoff with sensitivity and attention to communication (Noer, 1993).

Northern Digital by its actions had compromised trust and the possibility for communication at a time when they were needed the most. During a time of fear and uncertainty, when trust between people at different levels of the organization was acutely at risk, a powerful message had been broadcast: Do not speak up! A precious commodity—the valuing and acceptance of diversity—had been taken down a few notches, perhaps even crushed. Once again, a corporation had won in the legal arena, but it suffered a profound injury to its spirit and a loss of an opportunity for growth. This chapter's title, "A Modern Witch Hunt," suggests a drama with villains and victims. In truth, there are no villains in this piece. There are, however, many victims alongside the single employee whose career was ended. The deeper parallel with the witch trials of 400 years ago lies in the grim picture of a profound failure of leadership during a time of great turmoil, fear, and stress.

Lessons to Be Learned

Let us suppose for a moment that instead of rejoicing in the "victory" delivered by their lawyers, the executives of Northern Digital decided to see what could be learned from this painful and costly episode. What if they were to seize the opportunity to use this experience to become less "crisis prone?" Assuming this agreeable hypothetical, here are the lessons I would offer for their consideration.

Implement Your Violence Prevention Program
Through Training and Education

Northern Digital had a violence prevention program on the books, and there it stayed—thereby remaining totally useless. To be at all effective, a workplace violence policy must include clearly defined criteria for the behaviors that would fall under the policy. A set of procedures, including roles and responsibilities, must guide the actions of company personnel and to create clear expectations on the part of all employees about what to expect if a threat is reported or experienced. Neither of these essential components was in place. Behavioral expectations regarding threats and intimidation had not been communicated to employees at any level of the workforce. Even if these criteria had been clear to employees, they would have had no idea what procedure to follow in cases of suspected dangerousness. The employees who went to management with concerns about Norcross's behavior were prompted to do so not because of a company policy but because they had seen a program about workplace violence on television. It is clear that once the manager had been informed of the employees' concerns, he had no idea what to do. He improvised throughout, uncertain about procedures or principles to direct his actions.

Keep Upper Management Involved

In the absence of guidance to the contrary, George Kramer did what any middle manager would do in such a case: He handed the process down, rather than up. Rather than assemble the team, which would have included medical, legal, security, and human resources departments, and arrange to interview Norcross and other individuals who could provide useful information, company leadership allowed the process to be managed by individuals, acting alone and in an uncoordinated fashion. Kramer first handed the problem over to the medical department, where it was handled, or, more accurately, mishandled, by a line employee with no experience or training in handling workplace threats. This process was repeated in the security and human resources departments, where managers, inexperienced in their roles, untrained in handling situations of this kind, and lacking the guidance of corporate policy and procedures, fumbled in their attempts to assess the possible risk, to communicate information to the appropriate people in a timely way, and to manage decision making as the situation developed. All of this occurred without the involvement and awareness of corporate leadership at higher levels.

Stay in Touch With Your Employee

A hallmark characteristic of a crisis-prone organization is its failure to put concerns about human issues first. Although the company may have been correct in requiring Norcross to undergo a psychological evaluation once it determined that she had made the alleged statements, it mishandled the process. A psychological evaluation can be an intimidating, frightening experience, especially when your job may be on the line. It is crucial to help the employee feel as comfortable as possible with the process by staying in touch with him or her. Here, the opposite happened. In turning immediately to the medical department for guidance rather than first interviewing Norcross, management put the cart before the horse. Once Kramer was informed of the possible threat, he should have brought Norcross into the process as soon as possible. The first interview should have been conducted by company personnel with Norcross herself to make her aware of the nature of the allegations and to explain the process that would follow. The interview would have included a full explanation of issues concerning the evaluation, the disclosure of information and results, and the possible options following the results. Pam's informal lunch with her supervisor/friend was inadequate, confusing, and inappropriate. The medical department, for its part, compounded this problem by immediately turning the case over to outside professionals. Thus, the first actions in response to a warning involved a *distancing* of the company from the problem and from the employee herself, first from the management ranks to the medical department and then from the medical department to a professional outside the company entirely.

Be Prepared to Handle the Evaluation
Properly and Carefully

It is therefore not surprising that, appearing for the evaluation and confronted with a raft of legal forms, Norcross refused to comply. This is not the way to handle an employee suspected of violent or self-destructive potential. Good practice dictates that unless there is an acute situation (e.g., when a weapon is displayed or an immediate plan is expressed), the employee be approached directly by management and a face-to-face investigation be initiated. This first meeting also allows the employer to fully describe the evaluation process to the employee. This was not accomplished here. If it had been, Norcross might not have responded in the way that she did when confronted with a release form at the psychologist's office.

Even with the evaluation completed, however, management's actions in delegating the process down and outside the organization and the lack of coordination between departments caused serious and fateful gaps in the communication of the results. Crucial information was not shared in a timely fashion. The company, lacking procedure and guidelines, did not follow up in obtaining the results of the evaluation from the psychological contractor. Although the initial evaluation that was ordered by the medical department took place on a Thursday, 3 days later nothing had been communicated back to the medical department. Furthermore, following George's initial contact with Helen, communication between management and the human resources and medical departments about this crucial information was essentially nonexistent. This left human resources in the dark.

Don't Rely on Standard Medical Assessment Procedures

In the absence of direction from appropriate levels of company management, a line-level medical services employee was allowed total responsibility for determining procedure and policy in responding to a possible threat. As such, she fell back on standard, everyday procedures suited to a standard occupational health situation. The purpose of a typical occupational health assessment is to determine whether an individual who has been ill or has suffered an injury has recovered sufficiently to return to work. In the case of a possible threat, however, the question being asked is quite different; it bears directly on the safety of the employee and of the entire workplace. Clearly, the procedures governing standard evaluations are inappropriate and inadequate for such a task.

What should have happened instead? Management would have met directly with Norcross as the first step in a process of information gathering. If the facts merited—for example, if it were determined that she had in fact made the statements attributed to her—she would have been informed that as part of company policy she would be required to undergo an evaluation to determine if there was danger of violence. She would have been informed that the evaluation would be limited to this question alone and that the results with respect to the question of dangerousness would be shared with the company as well as with the employee herself. However, all of these steps were omitted. As a result, the employee was alienated and traumatized, the process was delayed, and crucial information was not communicated in time. If this had been a case where there was actual danger of violence, all of this could have significantly *increased* the risk that violence would occur.

Pay More Attention to How You Handle
a Security Investigation

Marian Ross was in her late 30s and had been the security manager for 2 years. Brought over from accounting, with no background in security or law enforcement, her training for the job consisted of 2 weeks of orientation before beginning the new position. She had no training or knowledge base in violence risk management. Furthermore, she was charged with "investigating" the Norcross threat with no guidance as to how to conduct a threat of violence investigation either from company leadership or from written policies. Without benefit of policies or the coordinated effort of a team, she was guided by her own interpretations and judgments. The inadequacies in the investigation were rife. For example, in her investigation, Marion did not investigate whether Norcross had any history of violent or threatening behavior. When asked in her deposition for an explanation for this omission, she stated, "That's not part of our policy on violence in the workplace." This explanation makes very little sense, for several reasons. First, there was no document addressing procedural issues such as how to conduct an investigation. Second, if there had been such a policy, it would certainly not have excluded a history of violence from a threat investigation. Clearly, there were no policies or procedures, and certainly there was no basis of experience or knowledge, to guide the investigation conducted by the security manager. Her input into the process of decision making was based as much on her impressions and biases as on facts. This makes even more poignant the statements on the part of the human resources department at the arbitration that "security was handling that" to explain the gaps in their own investigative activities.

Summary: This Can Happen to You!

A witch hunt happens when unfocused fear finds a target, often in some person or group that is different from the mainstream culture. The "witch" becomes the embodiment of that which is feared. In this case, as in many downsizing environments, what was feared is rage—the murderous, vengeful rage of the betrayed employee. In 17th-century Massachusetts, people who exhibited deviant personality styles, held radical religious beliefs, or were trapped in poverty were sometimes linked with satanic or destructive powers. Today, the feared quality is mental illness, which then becomes associated with the potential for violence. "Mental instability," "mood swings," "red flags": All are *code words* for the deviance that marks the modern witch for expulsion or punishment. Pam Norcross's deviance was her tendency to speak her feelings. In calmer, more secure times, this deviance had been tolerated. However, during a time of stress, the deviant behavior that had been tolerated in the past became an object of fear and a focus of aggression. Rumors were taken as fact. Norcross was deviant in one particular way. In other workplaces, we see others become the objects of fear and scrutiny: men who own guns, employees known to suffer from a mental illness, recent immigrant or minority groups entrants to the workforce, Vietnam veterans. Only strong leadership can offset the risks of a witch hunt. A story like this can be repeated in any company undergoing the stress of change.

The story of Northern Digital demonstrates dramatically the destructive effects of corporate fear and the importance of preserving the relationship with an employee suspected of or charged with making threats. When she said, "I would like to blow away that son of a bitch," Pam Norcross was voicing the rage of employees throughout the company for the disruption and sense of betrayal associated with the downsizing. The company's leadership feared that rage but was not able to confront it directly. When Pam gave voice to it, she became the focus of that fear. *This is a real risk in any downsizing environment.* The only way to ensure that this does not happen is to have procedures that ensure fairness and calm, reasoned information gathering and decision making. Otherwise, the witch hunt becomes a real possibility, perhaps even an inevitable outcome.

Note

1. In this case and in all subsequent case studies, fictitious names are used for companies and their employees.

When Systems Fail:

The Case of the Frightened Manager

It is our unseeingness that has permitted us to stumble so close to the abyss. . . . The withholding of knowledge and the unwillingness to draw conclusions from the knowledge we do possess add willful ignorance to willful blindness.

Lewis Mumford, *In the Name of Sanity*

This story is about corporate neglect and incompetence. It charts a pattern of escalating intimidation and threat that ultimately drove a talented manager from her job. Terrorized by a verbally and ultimately physically violent employee, this manager was failed first by her own employer and then by the legal system. It shows how an employer, by relying solely on legal principles to guide its response to a reported pattern of threat and assault, failed to protect its employee from that threat. It also provides a striking example of how the legal system often fails to hold corporations responsible for psychological injuries to employees.

55

June 1991

Anita Woodward[1] was an African American woman who had worked for Bosley Corporation (a Fortune 100 Company) for 7 years when she was promoted to supervisor of an important project. Anita was a bright engineer who welcomed the position of increased responsibility. Her promotion demonstrated that she had learned how to function in a profession dominated by males and in a corporate culture in which minorities faced particular challenges to being treated with respect. She was unprepared, however, for the challenge that awaited her following her promotion. Shortly after she assumed her new position, Anita was warned by her superior, Alan, that one of her subordinates, an engineer named Mahmet, was unhappy about being supervised by a woman and an African American. He told her that she would be well advised to do what she could to ease any tension that might arise between them.

Anita found that at first Mahmet was difficult to get along with. He challenged her continually, adopting a confrontational, often obstinate attitude about work assignments. However, Anita worked hard to improve the working relationship, paying extra attention to Mahmet and trying to avoid confrontation. For a period of time, this appeared to be successful, and the work proceeded with only an occasional confrontation or argument. Unknown to Anita, however, Mahmet had been making disparaging remarks about her to other members of the engineering staff. There were, however, no confrontations between the two.

January 1992

The situation changed dramatically when the time came for Mahmet's annual performance evaluation. Anita was prepared to give Mahmet an evaluation that noted several areas of performance as needing improvement. She discussed this with her superiors prior to meeting with Mahmet and learned that prior supervisors had rated his performance as poor. At the evaluation meeting, he become hostile and aggressive with her, demanding that she change the evaluation and recommend him for a promotion. After this, he become markedly more difficult to get along with, not only with Anita but with other project engineers as well. Anita and her superior had to talk with him several times about his hostile and uncooperative behavior toward his coworkers.

Over the next several months, several other incidents occurred.

March 1992

Anita's supervisor asked her to obtain some information from Mahmet about an aspect of the project for which he was responsible. When she spoke to Mahmet about this, he became very upset, used obscene language about the supervisor, and said, "I'll get my gun and blow his head off."

June 1992

Several engineers had complained to Anita's superior about Mahmet's behavior toward coworkers. They had reported that he was often surly and uncooperative. Besides being unpleasant, this was interfering with their ability to perform their work. Because a deadline was looming and they were all under pressure to perform for this important client, these engineers had appealed to Alan to correct the situation as soon as possible. Alan documented the complaints and requested that Anita talk with Mahmet about them. When Anita did so, Mahmet became very angry, claiming that it was "none of her business" what went on between him and other engineers. When Anita replied that she had the right to speak to him about issues that directly affected the performance of the work group, he suddenly rose from his chair and shouted, "If you call me a slave again I will kick your ass." Anita ended the meeting and reported the incident to Alan. No action was taken by company management to respond to this reported behavior.

September 1992

Anita received an excellent evaluation and a one-grade promotion. Although she kept this information to herself, Mahmet told her that he had "connections" that had informed him of her promotion. He told her that the only reason she was promoted was that she was black and a woman.

October 1992

Alan asked Anita to assign additional work to Mahmet that would require him to work out of the office for a week. Mahmet refused this assignment. Anita arranged that they meet with her manager to discuss it further. During this meeting,

Mahmet became agitated and appeared to be very angry with Anita. After the meeting concluded, Anita was walking down the hall when Mahmet approached her from the opposite direction. She later reported that he had a "look of rage in his eyes" and that she was frightened. As he passed by her, he jabbed his elbow into her, hurting her. As he did this, he said to her, "Look out, man, somebody could get hurt." Anita immediately reported this assault to Alan. He said he would discuss the matter with human resources and get back to her.

The next day, Alan called Anita and told her that Mahmet had been informed that if he threatened Anita in any way he would be terminated. However, Anita would have to continue to work with him. Anita contacted human resources manager Barbara Golden to find out what could be done to protect her from any future assaults from Mahmet. Barbara told her that all she could do was to keep a log of any further incidents.

October 1992 to February 1993

Although there were no further overt incidents over the next few months, and although Anita had no contact with Mahmet, several developments increased her feelings of discomfort and threat. The department secretary told her that on several occasions Mahmet had asked her where Anita was. On at least two occasions, Anita observed Mahmet simply standing around the parking garage near where she parked her car. Around this time, Fred, the project manager, told Anita that he thought that Mahmet had a problem with being supervised by a woman. He also told her that he had known Mahmet for a long time and that he thought Mahmet might be "schizophrenic or psychotic."

March 15, 1993

It was time for Anita to present Mahmet with his annual performance review. Because of the situation, Alan was present for the meeting. As Mahmet read his evaluation, he became extremely angry and threatening toward Anita. He said that he felt that Anita was using the evaluation to hurt him personally and stated, "You won't get away with what you are trying to do to me." Following this meeting, Anita was so upset that she began crying. She told Alan that this was only the last straw in the series of intimidations (including the one physical assault) that had taken place over the last 18 months. Alan suggested that Anita go home. She had to be escorted to her car because she was afraid to walk to the parking garage alone. That evening, Alan called Anita at home and informed her that Mahmet would be removed from the project, but only when the company found another project for him.

March 17, 1993

Anita returned to work, but she was so frightened that her husband had to escort her to the office. She met with Alan and told him that she no longer felt safe coming to work. Alan agreed that she was owed a safe working environment. He arranged a meeting with his immediate superior to discuss the situation. He explained the history of the situation and reiterated his wish that Mahmet be off the project as soon as possible. About 2 weeks later, Anita learned that Mahmet had been promised a supervisory position on another project. He had not been disciplined in any way for his behavior.

April 8, 1993

Dave, another engineer on Anita's project, warned her that Mahmet was "out to get her, no matter what it took." He told her to be careful. Helen, a supervisor on the project, confirmed what Dave had said. She told Anita that Mahmet had made the threat in her presence, saying that "he would not go down alone" and that "he would do whatever he had to do to ensure that." Helen told Anita that she believed that Mahmet was serious about doing physical harm to her, that she thought he was dangerous, and that Anita should be very careful. However, Helen told Anita that she was not willing to repeat this to management, for fear that Mahmet would retaliate against her.

Very frightened, Anita immediately went to Alan and his manager, Betty, to inform them of what she had just learned. Alan and Betty talked with human resources and with someone in the corporate office of general counsel "to make sure they were handling the situation correctly." Alan then called Anita and told her that unless the person who had given her the information would come forward, the company could do nothing to protect her. He also told her that if she had "officially documented" the hitting incident, they would have been in a position to terminate Mahmet. Anita told Alan that she had understood that all that was necessary to "document" the incident was to report it to her supervisor. She repeated to Alan that she was frightened and seriously concerned about her safety.

April 9, 1993

The next day, Anita could not go to work. Alan called her at home, and she told him that she was so frightened and stressed that she was not sure that she could function at the workplace.

April 11, 1993

Alan, Betty, and Barbara phoned Anita, who was still staying away from the workplace. They told her that they had arranged for her to meet with a counselor from the Employee Assistance Program to help her "deal with the stress." They reiterated that unless the person with the information came forward, they could not discharge Mahmet.

April 14, 1993

Anita, accompanied by her husband, met with Alan, Mahmet, Fred (Mahmet's manager), and Barbara. Anita explained to them that the situation had begun to affect her health and that she was experiencing headaches, upset stomach, and sleeplessness. She repeated that unless something was done, she felt that it was unsafe for her to return to work. Barbara told her that the company would not terminate Mahmet because they were concerned that he would sue the company for wrongful termination.

April 24, 1993

Ten days later, Anita resigned from the company. In a brief letter to Alan, she wrote the following:

For the past year, Mahmet has been very hostile, obstinate and violent towards me. . . . During this time he has made many statements to me using vulgar language, made threats to me, hit me on the arm in the work place, attempted to assassinate my character professionally and recently told a project team member of his intent to do physical harm to me. These incidents have caused me to fear for my safety in the workplace and have made it extremely difficult to function effectively because of the unsafe work environment.

As you know, these incidents have been reported to the proper project and functional managers. However, the proper action was not taken against Mahmet to ensure this type of behavior would cease. Therefore, this situation got increasingly worse and unbearable for me. No employee should be confronted with threatening comments and gestures in the work place. Yet this was allowed to happen to me. Given the options available to me at this time, I have no other recourse than to terminate my employment to ensure my safety and well being.

April 30, 1993, to May 6, 1993

Anita's resignation gained the attention of management at higher levels and jolted the company into action. About a week after her resignation, Anita received a letter from a senior human resources manager. In the letter, he asked her to reconsider her resignation, offering her a paid leave of absence with generous terms. The letter began the process of reconstructing the facts of how the company had handled Anita's concerns over the past year and a half. In it, the manager assured Anita that "the incidents described in your letter are issues that the company has treated very seriously." He went on to say that

> given the information available to your management in October, 1992 and April, 1993, action was taken and alternatives and/or solutions were discussed with you in an effort to resolve all of your concerns. In addition, Mahmet was counseled and given a verbal warning subsequent to the elbow incident and he was removed from the Pearson Project and reassigned to a project located in another building.

Finally, the manager informed her that the company had now hired independent experts to come to the workplace to evaluate the situation and requested her participation in being interviewed by these workplace violence specialists. Anita refused to cooperate with the investigation in any way. In a telephone conversation with the human resources manager, she expressed her desire that the company proceed to process her resignation. In a follow-up letter, the manager accepted her resignation. He also informed her that the consultants had completed their work and that they were "unable to identify any evidence that a threat exists toward you or any other member of the project team."

July 1995 to May 1995

Anita retained an attorney and filed a lawsuit against Bosley Corporation for discrimination, intentional infliction of emotional distress, failure to maintain a safe work environment, and negligent hiring, supervision, and retention. The original petition stated that "the Defendant breached this duty [to provide a safe work environment] by either intentionally or negligently permitting Mahmet to engage in an ongoing pattern of misconduct which included discrimination, harassment, retaliation, assault, battery and intentional infliction of emotional distress against Plaintiff." During the summer, the discovery stage of the case proceeded. Depositions were held by both sides, and Anita's attorney prepared her case. The attorney contacted me, requesting that I serve as an expert witness. After reviewing the records that the attorney sent me, I agreed, telling the lawyer that I felt without a doubt that the company had injured Anita by its mishandling of the situation. In my written opinion, I stated that the symptoms experienced by Anita and her subsequent resignation were the direct result of the threats and of the company's failure to take action to protect her. Meanwhile, the company's lawyers submitted a motion for summary judgment to the U.S. District Court. If granted, the motion would essentially say to Anita that she did not have a case and that it would not be considered by the court. On May 1, the judge granted the company's motion for summary judgment. In her decision, the judge held that the plaintiff's claims did not fulfill the criteria required by existing legal precedents. She did not reference my statement, medical records, and the issue of psychological harm to Anita. The case was over, never to be tried.

Lessons to Be Learned

Once again, I had seen a large corporation charged with damaging an employee by mishandling a threat situation. Once again, I had seen the company "prevail" in the legal arena. Obviously, along with her lawyers, I felt that the legal system had failed Anita. But it had also failed Bosley Corporation. "Case closed," I imagined the executives and attorneys saying, "Crisis resolved." We know that this is far from the truth, however. Faced with mounting indications of a highly stressful and possibly unsafe situation, the corporation was unable to respond effectively. As a result, it lost an employee and exposed itself to a lawsuit. In addition, it created an atmosphere of mistrust and fear that may have infected other employees as well, undermining confidence in leadership and decreasing productivity and morale. Far from having resolved the policy and practice issues that emerged here, the company had succeeded only in worsening its deeply rooted crisis-prone tendencies. "Winning" the case would serve only to reinforce the blindness and arrogance that had created the crisis and caused the loss of Anita. Whether or not Bosley Corporation ever reverses this trend—and the chances are very good that more "opportunities" to learn from mistakes will occur—we can learn much from this story. Several issues emerge clearly.

Lack of Guiding Policy

This case provides another example of how dangerous and destructive it can be for a company to function without a specific policy to govern threats of violence. Beyond the facts of this particular situation, however, we must ask, What does this lack of policy indicate about the culture of this company in general? The lack of response to Anita's situation is hard to understand on the basis of common sense and simply good practice about acceptable behavior in the workplace. Was the absence of a policy just one indication of a culture that was oblivious to human concerns? Clearly, the corporation was unprepared to deal with reports of harassment and threat that were coming in, not only from Anita, but from other managers. One wonders about the corporation's record in general in responding to reports of mistreatment, harassment, or threat.

Lack of Special Procedures

One indication of this lack of attention to behavioral and climate problems was the apparent absence of procedures to guide response to potentially disruptive or unhealthy situations. Despite repeated reports of Mahmet's problematic behavior, committed in the context of a history of poor performance, the company handled the reports of his abusive and disruptive behavior toward his supervisor and coworkers like any standard performance or discipline problem: It was handed off to his immediate supervisor for correction. This, therefore, is a case that demonstrates powerfully the need for a team and other alternative approaches to problem solving when a violence threat is reported. If, for example, an investigation early in the process revealed that Mahmet was an unhappy, problematic employee who was claiming that he was being evaluated unfairly, this should have been flagged as a sign of trouble and taken up directly in a meeting involving human resources and his managers. If coworkers felt that Mahmet was hard to work with, this could have been assessed on a groupwide basis and solutions proposed. If there were communication problems between Mahmet and Anita as his supervisor, a team could have been tasked with seeking methods to resolve it through mediation or alternate dispute resolution. Here is yet another example of the limits of standard disciplinary and employee relations procedures for dealing with conflict and threats. Clearly, no such procedures existed, and no such resources were considered.

Resort to a Legal Approach

Approaching the problem through standard disciplinary means only made the problem worse. In time, an irritant become a crisis. And as such it revealed the reactive crisis management style of the company. Now in early crisis mode, Bosley Corporation did what many crisis-prone companies do: It retreated to a defensive, legalistic posture. The call to the corporate headquarters appears to have produced just such a response: "There is nothing we can do if the informant refuses to come forward." But this response makes no sense in the context of events. When the person at headquarters said to the manager that there was nothing that could be done unless the person reporting the threat came forward, what legal principle was being followed? Did it have to do with protecting the company from possible litigation from Mahmet for bringing unsupported charges? Did it come from concerns about protecting Mahmet's privacy, again revealing concerns about protecting the company from future action by Mahmet?

This retreat to legal defensiveness is common where there is an absence of policies and procedures to deal with situations involving aberrant or disruptive behavior. In this case, good practice and common sense would have dictated that, faced with these allegations and reports, the company follow up by seeking more information. What it actually did was use legal principles to *avoid* action. This is not to say that attention to employment law is wrong in these circumstances; to the contrary, it is crucial. In fact, the company in its actions evidenced considerable *ignorance* of employment law principles. For example, the company should have known, or been advised, that the duty to provide a safe workplace would have required decisive, prompt action to pursue all legal avenues of information gathering. Furthermore, established principles and practices were available to guide them in *legally* pursuing an investigation while respecting and preserving Mahmet's privacy. These would include limiting the scope of the investigation to those people thought to have relevant information, involving only those staff with a crucial role and enjoining them to keep their knowledge of the investigation and the case confidential, and sharing information frugally with interviewees on a strictly "need-to-know" basis. Finally, they would be advised to carefully document all their activities so that they could be justified in case of a future challenge to legality or appropriateness.

Reliance on Discipline as the Sole Response

The company managers were, curiously, stuck on the notion that the company had to discipline or even terminate Mahmet because of what Anita was telling them. The company's preoccupation with issues of "evidence" in relation to the informant who would not come forward and the concern about Mahmet suing them for wrongful termination suggests that it felt pushed to act in a certain way by Anita's allegations. This was putting the cart before the horse. The employer's responsibility, once the reports began coming in, was simply to conduct its own investigation, with or without the help of consultants in the initial stages. It was simply a question of looking into a situation that appeared to compromise the safety of the workplace and perhaps requiring, once the facts were established, an administrative action that might include discipline or termination. But because the company did not understand this responsibility and the steps that it required, it limited its response to the situation to considerations of discipline. In doing so, the company effectively acted *as if no threat existed.* The primary issue, that of Anita's safety and her growing fear that she would be harmed, was *never* the subject of discussion or action until after she resigned in desperation.

Referral to the Employee Assistance Program for Counseling

This is a classic example of the misuse of counseling services. What was required here was decisive administrative action, beginning with an investigation of the facts, not a feeble offer of counseling to the victim to help her "deal with her stress." This is blaming the victim in the classic sense. It was, further, yet another way that the company attempted to shift responsibility onto Anita and away from itself. When it made that offer, the company was saying, in the clearest possible terms, "The problem is in you and in your reaction to these events. It is up to you to fix the problem."

Calling in a Violence Consultant
After the Damage Was Done

The consultant was called in too late to be of assistance. The company's timing in hiring the consultant would raise questions of credibility and good faith in even the most gullible and naive of observers. Given the behavior of the company up to the point of Anita's resignation, calling for a consultant appeared to be motivated by fear for itself rather than by concern for the employee. Furthermore, it was too late from a practical standpoint. Anita, hurt, frustrated, and alienated by the employer's poor handling of the situation, had already left the boundaries of the workplace emotionally. Now that the employer was finally saying, "You have our attention, please work with us to solve this problem," she was saying, "It's too late. I don't trust you. There is no more 'we.'"

Inadequate, Biased Consultation

Dr. R., the head of the violence consulting firm, prepared a declaration as part of the discovery process when the legal case was initiated. After first establishing his credentials as a workplace violence expert, Dr. R. described that he was engaged by the company in May 1993 to investigate Anita's complaints about Mahmet's threats. He explained that he and an associate spent 3 days interviewing workers and managers but that they were unable to interview Anita because she was unwilling to participate. He wrote that they had offered to see her at home but that she was "unwilling to participate even with a home interview." The use of the word *even* betrays Dr. R.'s bias in favor of the company's position and suggests his inability to understand or represent Anita's point of view. He then went on to offer two conclusions:

> First, Bosley management personnel evidenced a balanced and appropriate concern for the rights of both employees, and sought to provide prompt access to all employees who might have potentially useful information in this matter. They were organized, uniformly cooperative in the investigation process, and responded promptly to requests to collect relevant information. Second, there was no evidence present to support the premise that Mahmet posed a threat of harm to Anita or any other employee.

From the first conclusion, it is clear that the consultant is talking about the company's cooperation with *the consultant's investigation.* There is no reference to or discussion of the company's actions *before* Anita's resignation and the hiring of the outside specialist. This is a crucial omission. A threat-of-violence investigation is a complex endeavor that must take into account factors and circumstances over time and on a system level. Dr. R.'s investigation was grievously limited by the lack of access to Anita and by the omission of any consideration of the actions of the company in relation to her during the entire 18-month period in which she supervised Mahmet. It is not hard to understand that Bosley's leadership cooperated fully with Dr. R. once Anita's resignation had secured their attention. What is of interest here is the contrast between the level of attention and activity after her resignation and the neglect, denial, and lack of coordination that led up to Anita's inability to function on the job and her decision to resign.

But the company was not asking the consultant to evaluate actions taken prior to Anita's resignation, and these questions are not addressed or answered by Dr. R. Although the consultant's declaration mentions 3 days of interviews and the collection of "relevant information," there is no reference to notes, records, or information to examine the company's response to the situation from its beginnings. We can assume, therefore, that an examination of the company's response to Anita's cries for help was not a part of the investigation. The purpose of the investigation was to "clean up" the mistake and protect the company from the appearance of wrongdoing in relation to Anita rather than a genuine self-examination leading to learning or to an attempt to repair the damage to the relationship with Anita. The work of the consultant thus served to support the company's damaging position here and to reinforce the mistake. The subsequent legal "victory" probably ensured that a self-examination never took place.

One must also ask: If the consultants conducted such a thorough evaluation—and two consultants for 3 days should have indeed been sufficient—why did they not come across the employees who had reported Mahmet's threatening behavior to Anita? Could it have been that, in the climate of mistrust and fear that existed, those employees chose to keep silent to consultants they perceived to be agents of the company? Perhaps other employees, observing what had happened to Anita, realized that this was a place where "blowing the whistle" on violence and harassment was not a wise course of action.

The report of the consultant reflected the poorly timed and misdirected actions of the employer. First, the fact that the employer waited until Anita had left the workplace had a crucial effect on the ability of the consultant to achieve the primary goal, which was a response to Anita's concerns. Faced with the task of evaluating whether a threat existed, the hired experts had no access to the most important set of facts, which was the experience of the person who felt threatened. Furthermore, without benefit of Anita's input, the consultant had access to only one side of the story and was unable to gain a total understanding of the situation. As such, the report was essentially a whitewash. Far from helping achieve a resolution of the problem or helping those involved learn from the experience, the consultants were drawn into a collusion with the company's defensive reconstruction of the entire case.

The Big Picture: Are We Being Fair?

In this case, like that of Northern Digital, the laws designed to protect employee rights actually served to shield the employer from liability. In both cases, an arbitrator or judge ruled in favor of the employer, stating that the plaintiff/ employee had failed to establish discrimination according to criteria established by statute or precedent. This case shows how the legal structure shields companies from liability for hurting employees. "But that's only fair," some corporate executives may protest, "given how we are held hostage to employment law in this land of employment at will! We daily walk through a minefield of laws and regulations designed to protect employees, any of which are constantly used against us by unhappy or difficult workers. So I won't cry about it when a law serves to shield me from liability!" This is an understandable but misguided attitude. These cases demonstrate how the law can be used as a weapon in an unnecessary and destructive war. When laws are used solely as a defense, they replace the search for tools for understanding and real solutions to the problems that underlie these disputes. The laws are important and serve a useful purpose. But we must go beyond the letter of the law to the spirit of collaboration and crisis prevention. Reliance on the law, and on a defensive, legalistic approach, makes a company crisis prone. It sets the stage for more trouble.

Could the company have proceeded in a more positive manner while still preserving its legal options? Close attention to employment law issues is an important part of good practice in these cases. But a narrow, rigid use of one legal principle is not good practice. The risk that Mahmet would accuse the company of invasion of privacy or discrimination had to be balanced against the damage that could be done if the charges against him were true. As long as issues of privacy were considered in the action plan, questions of possible discrimination were considered, and this process was documented fully, the company could have and should have proceeded to directly investigate the reports of his behavior.

What is the truth? Was Mahmet a danger to Anita? Because of the way in which this story unfolded, we will never know the answer to this question. The consultant agreed to render an opinion without interviewing Anita. Therefore, the conclusion about threat was based on the report of the alleged threatener as well as other people in the workplace. It is not clear if the woman who informed Anita of the verbal threats by Mahmet was interviewed or, if she was, that she told what she knew. The consultant's conclusion that "there was no evidence present to support the premise that Mahmet posed a threat of harm to Ms. Woodward" is true on the face of it. In fact, however, the most relevant "evidence" in the case was never considered: Anita's experience of the company's abuse and neglect.

There are other important unanswered questions raised by this case, which are ultimately more important than the now moot question of whether Anita was actually in danger. These are questions that relate to the company's failure to respond to an employee's report that she *felt* threatened. This story ends with the legal system supporting the company's position that it did nothing wrong. But is this the end of the story for Bosley Corporation and others like it? What are the real costs of institutionalized, corporate neglect of basic human issues? How would you feel about working for this corporation? What kind of image does this company present to its own people and to the community at large? What employee of this company would ever feel safe enough to bring instances of harassment, threat, or abuse to a corporate level? In fact, it is impossible to calculate the costs of "winning" this case for the executives of Bosley. And the most profound and potentially costly fact of all is that, having won in the courts, no one inside that company is currently asking that question.

Note

1. The names of individuals and of the company have been changed and some circumstances disguised to protect privacy. Except for names, however, letters and other documents are quoted verbatim.

7

"Doesn't He Fit the Profile?"

The Case of Roger

We are used to thinking of compassion as an emotional state, based on
our concern for one another. But it is also grounded in a level of
awareness. . . . As people see more of the systems in which they
operate, and as they understand more clearly the pressures influencing
one another, they naturally develop more compassion and empathy.
Peter Senge, *The Fifth Discipline*

This is a success story.

A Loose Cannon in the Mortgage Department

I was called by Susan, the human resources director of a medium-sized retail bank. She told me that she had a situation that was causing great concern and that she needed guidance about what to do. Roger had worked in the mortgage-processing department for a little less than 2 years. He had been an average performer, clearly capable but a bit erratic and sometimes "touchy" in his dealings with other people. Lately, the bank had been pushing to increase the volume of mortgage business, and there had been pressure on this small department to move applications along more quickly. Some thought that the pressure was having a negative effect on Roger. Coworkers reported that he was complaining that he was being pushed too hard and had seemed to be holding up some of the work needlessly. Most of the other clerks in the department were young women—Roger was in his late 30s and single—and several had reported being uncomfortable with him. In fact, several months earlier, just before Roger's performance review, one of the women, Janice, had come to Susan and said that one day, Roger flew into one of his "rages." She said that this was something he would do from time to time, whenever the pressure got to him. But this time was different because he seemed more frustrated than usual and said, "If you see me come in one day in my fatigues with my Uzi, you'll know to hit the deck." Because she was afraid of Roger's temper, Janice asked Susan that they not tell Roger that she had reported this incident. Susan agreed and conferred with Roger's supervisor about how to raise the issue in Roger's upcoming review without compromising Janice. At the review, which occurred the next week, they included language that vaguely referred to "inappropriate interaction with peers that was causing a tense environment within the department." In another oblique reference to the reported threat, Roger's supervisor also noted that she "explained to Roger that what he may consider humorous others may consider inappropriate in an business environment." Roger was unhappy with his review and said that he did not understand what was being referred to about his interpersonal behavior.

Things were quiet until June, when a second serious incident provoked the call to me. Roger had returned from a weekend away in which his car had broken down and he had been stranded out of town. He returned angry and on edge. In the cafeteria at lunchtime, he told coworkers about his experience. Someone tried to cheer him up by joking goodnaturedly about similar car "horror stories." Apparently, Roger was upset by what was said, feeling that people were ridiculing him. One of the employees involved in the lunchtime conversation was Bill, who was in charge of building maintenance. Later, after hours when the building was almost empty, Bill encountered Roger in the elevator, on his way out of the building. Roger suddenly appeared to lose control, and, pinning Bill against the side of the elevator and with a wild look in his eyes, told him that if he ever talked to Roger like that again, he would kill him. Shaken, Bill reported this to Ed, the vice president, early the following day. Ed took this to Susan, who then called me. "Oh, by the way," Susan said to me, as she completed this recounting, "Roger often wears military fatigues and dogtags to work, even though we think he has never been in the military. He's sort of strange, and a loner, isn't that some sort of a profile? Should we be concerned?"

The profile, indeed! Was this not the "classic" picture of the violent employee: white male, single, loner, with a paranoid-sounding thinking style and a bad temper? And did the military dress carry with it a fascination with weaponry? I told Susan that on the basis of his behavior alone there was definitely cause for concern and that they needed to respond to Roger's behavior directly and imme- diately. However, even in the face of this frightening constellation of signs, we were not yet able to form an opinion about whether any actual danger existed. We would have to determine what, if any, real threat was posed by Roger. In addition, the company would have to respond immediately to the concerns of the employees who had been affected by Roger's threats and his disruptive behavior. I proposed that I meet with him to perform a dangerousness assessment. First, however, it would be necessary for them to meet with Roger themselves.

Meeting With the Employee

It was important that Susan and Ed do this before Roger was introduced to me. Roger had to be confronted about his behavior by the employer directly. He had to hear from them that these reports were being made and that the behavior was unacceptable, in direct violation of rules and policies, and could carry consequences with respect to his employment. (We acknowledged that the first opportunity to do that had been missed several months ago.) It would be Roger's right as an employee to respond to the reports and to be informed of the procedure that would be followed. As part of my role in assessing dangerousness, I too would ask him about this behavior, but my goals were different, and the process I would follow would be different. My contact with him could not take the place of an initial and direct discussion with his employer.

As we have seen in many of the cases presented in this book, all too often employers faced with a possible threat of violence send the employee directly off to a third party to participate in an unfamiliar, intimidating process. This leaves the employee feeling confused and threatened himself. It thus carries several disad- vantages. First, if the employee is indeed dangerous, it may increase the risk because it increases his sense of isolation, mistrust, and helplessness, which are all conditions that we know contribute directly to the threat of violence. Employees at risk for violence, or who are behaving in a threatening manner, need first and foremost an experience of *direct contact* with the employer. The second disadvantage is that it limits the quality of information. We want to know first how the offending employee will respond to a direct inquiry from the employer when he is confronted with the facts that are known to that point. This information is infinitely preferable to whatever story the employee may present to a doctor, who the employee knows is there to evaluate his mental health, dangerousness, and overall fitness to remain an employee; the employee sees this encounter, quite accurately, as a test, not as an opportunity for dialogue. Once the employee has had that initial contact with the employer, the assessment interview to follow will have a better chance of success. Importantly, one of the purposes of the meeting with the employer is to inform the employee about the purpose of the meeting with the doctor/specialist, the procedures that will safeguard his privacy, the methods by which information will be shared, and the decision-making process that will ensue.

Looking After the Others

Prior to their meeting with Roger, Mary and Ed needed to inform Janice and Bill that they would be following up on their reports immediately with an investigation. In doing so, they had to repair the mistake that had been made several months earlier when they neglected to confront the incident with Janice directly. This is another common mistake regarding threats. Employees who come forward with information about possible threats must be informed that, as in cases of sexual harassment, every effort will be made to protect informants, but that once the information has been shared, it must be followed up. In the case of sexual harassment, this is a matter of law. In the case of violence, it is a matter of both safety and legal protection. With respect to safety, common sense dictates that although an employer must make an effort to protect informants, no one, including the informant, is safe when this kind of report is buried or responded to in the vague, ineffective way that this one was initially handled. Regarding legal protection, the tort of negligent retention clearly comes into play when an employer fails to take action in response to knowledge of possible dangerousness. In other words, once the employer is informed of a threat or of the possibility of dangerousness, the employer must take action that is in proportion to the seriousness of the report. These principles need to be made matters of company policy so that no ambiguity or possibility for individual "judgment calls" exists when reports of threat or dangerousness occur.

Janice and Bill were informed of what was to take place. They accepted the necessity of this and appeared relieved. They were also informed that as part of the investigation process, they would be meeting with me. They were reassured that as information was gathered, their safety and that of all other employees would be the primary concern, and that they would be informed and action taken if and when there was any concern about their safety. We arranged for a security guard to be stationed in the next room while the meeting with Roger took place. Ed and Susan would meet with Roger that morning. They would begin by informing him that they were meeting with him because of the reports that they had received about his threatening behavior. They would describe both incidents and inform him that, regardless of whether he had had any intention to actually harm his coworkers, any such verbal threat or physically threatening behavior was a serious breach of the rules. They would tell him that although administrative or disciplinary action could certainly result, that no decision was being made at this point, pending the results of the investigation. As part of the investigation, a specialist would meet with him and with other employees. Following these interviews, Ed and Susan would meet with Roger again to discuss the findings and next steps. They would emphasize to him that he was not being fired or disciplined at this point but that given the seriousness of the reports and the risks involved, his continued employment was contingent on his participation in this procedure. The interviews would begin immediately, and until a resolution had been reached, he would be placed on a paid administrative leave.

First Contact With Roger

Susan and Ed met with Roger in Susan's office. The bank's security officer was stationed discreetly in the room next door. At the same time, I met in a nearby office with Bill and then with Janice, and with another female employee who worked closely with Roger, who Mary felt would be eager to talk with me and would have useful information and impressions to share. Roger's meeting with Ed and Susan was interesting. He was mystified and surprised by the reports. Although he remembered the incidents in question, he denied having made the threatening statements attributed to him. In fact, he had no memory of any statements that could have been experienced as threatening. He understood the procedure that was described to him. According to Susan and Ed's later description of the meeting,

Roger seemed calm, engaged, and accepting of the need to pursue these reports. He agreed to meet with me. My interviews with Ed and with Roger's coworkers yielded a picture of a socially uncomfortable and immature young man who was quick to take offense but who generally suppressed his anger until it erupted in unpredictable outbursts. Although they did not imagine him capable of violence, they were afraid of his emotional volatility and did not rule out the possibility that he might present a danger to them if he were to "snap."

I Meet Roger

Roger entered the interview with me initially mistrustful and guarded. He was of slight build and appeared considerably younger than his 37 years. Roger seemed mystified by what had happened that morning. When I assured him that it was not my job to decide whether he would keep his job, he relaxed and eventually became quite forthcoming. I said that my main purpose was to listen to what he had to say and that I was interested in a wide range of information about his background, his experience at work in general, and his general life and functioning. Typically, employees in this kind of situation either acknowledge that they made the statements attributed to them but assert that these were made in jest or taken out of context or too literally or state that they were grossly misquoted or their words distorted. Roger, however, as he had to his employers earlier, claimed that he had no memory of doing the things that had been described. I believed him. I began to wonder if he had some kind of psychological or neurological condition that produced emotional states or explosive reactions that were out of his control and were dissociated from his everyday consciousness. This might explain his lack of memory for these incidents. When he told me about his earlier life, including what sounded like an undetected learning disability, a history of failures at school, and disapproval from his parents, I began to suspect more strongly the presence of neurological and psychological impairments that could contribute to chronic problems with stress, relationships, and anger management.

I also specifically asked Roger about any history of violent behavior or thinking, or any history of being abused or exposed to violence at home or elsewhere. I asked him if he had any current violent thoughts or plans and if he owned or had access to weapons of any kind. I asked him about suicidality, depression, irrational thoughts, auditory hallucinations (hearing voices), or any history of treatment for psychological problems or symptoms. He answered all in the negative.

When I shared with Roger my thoughts that perhaps he had been struggling for most of his life with learning and intellectual performance issues and that this might be causing him stress at work, he agreed enthusiastically and appreciatively; it was as if a light had been turned on for him. I told him that there might be a need to do some more exploration about what had been going on for him but that I thought that the trouble he was in, and the outbursts that had been reported by others, might be related to these long-term issues. I told Roger I would share my observations to this point with his employers so that they could make a decision about the next steps in this process. I explained that once I did this, he would meet with Ed and Susan again. He was comfortable with this.

Recommendations to Management

I asked Roger to wait while I spoke with Ed and Susan. I shared my observations and hunches with them and made the following recommendations:

1. It was my opinion that there was no imminent risk of violence. However, given Roger's recent behavior and his unawareness and apparent inability to control these behaviors, his presence created an atmosphere of threat that was unhealthy for his work group and ultimately for the entire workplace. If the benefit structure allowed, through medical leave, use of vacation time, or a combination, Roger should be allowed to remain employed and receive his salary but not return to work at this time. Because I felt that the assessment process might require an extended period of time, I did not recommend a paid administrative leave.

2. Decisions about discipline or continued employment should be deferred pending the results of Recommendation 3.

3. During this time, Roger should undergo a specialized neuropsychological evaluation to determine the presence of specific cognitive and neurological impairments, as well as to provide a complete personality assessment and profile. This evaluation should also include a vocational assessment. Together, these results would help determine what kinds of employment suited Roger best and would guide recommendations regarding his suitability for his current employment. Because the employer was requesting this assessment for the purpose of aiding in the decision regarding Roger's future with the bank, and because the assessment results and report would be the property of the bank, the employer should pay for this assessment.

4. I also recommended that I meet with Roger several times during the weeks that this process was going on. This would provide support for him and allow me to monitor his condition. Collaborating with the specialist who would

perform the neuropsychological and career assessment, I would also interpret the results to Roger when the assessment was completed, as well as sharing with him what recommendations I would be making to the bank.

5. At the conclusion of the assessment, Ed and Susan would meet with Roger to discuss the recommendations and their decision regarding his employment. I also recommended that one or both of them meet briefly with the employees in Roger's department to inform them that Roger would be absent from the workplace for a time. They would be told that out of consideration for Roger's privacy they would not know more than this but that they be assured that their safety was the paramount concern and that if there were any information that involved their safety, they would be informed and action would be taken to protect them.

Ed and Susan accepted these recommendations. They met with Roger in my presence and presented all of this to him. They requested that he refrain from coming to the workplace (except, of course, to the retail lobby of the bank to transact business like any other customer) and that he restrict any necessary telephone contacts to Mary. I would be in touch with Roger to arrange the assessment and to meet with him periodically. We estimated for him that the process would require from 2 to 4 weeks. At its conclusion, I would meet with Roger to share the results of the assessment with him. I would also share the results with the bank, and he would then meet with Susan and Ed to discuss their decision about his employment.

Results of the Evaluation

Roger underwent a complete psychological and career assessment evaluation as planned. The results supported my hunch and provided useful insights into the source of Roger's difficulties. Roger had a marked deficit in brain functioning in the areas of memory, information processing, and, interestingly, registration of facial expressions and emotional cues. In effect, Roger had a learning disability that had affected his performance in a wide range of cognitive tasks from childhood on but that had never before been identified. In the opinion of the psychologist, Roger's deficit definitely interfered with his ability to perform his job. Roger could not have chosen a job that would be harder with respect to challenging this handicap. Although he had managed to compensate for his handicap, his frustration and sheer stress would periodically surface, especially when the pressure was on high. Furthermore, his deficits in processing interpersonal cues had, over time, contributed to severe unease with people and a crushing sense of inferiority. Roger's high vulnerability to stress, worsened by the demands of his job, had combined with his problems interacting with people and his low self-esteem to produce these frightening outbursts. The psychologist concluded that it would be in Roger's best interests to reevaluate his career path in the light of these results and to enter into counseling to resolve the emotional issues that had resulted from his undetected disability.

I presenting these results to Ed and Mary. After considering these results, they decided not to continue Roger's employment. They felt that, given what had happened, it would be impossible for Roger to comfortably reenter the workplace. Roger was actually quite happy with this decision. After reading the report, he felt that it was best for him to take some time away from the demands of a job and reevaluate his life and his career plans. He returned to his family home in a nearby state. Equipped with this new information about himself, he was now prepared to make choices that would set him on a successful path.

Lessons Learned

When we consider this case, one simple but overwhelming fact stands out: Although ultimately Roger was fired for making threatening statements in the workplace, *he left feeling wonderful about the employer.* How was this accomplished? Here was a case that was, at first hearing, every employer's nightmare. An employee had made direct threats. His behavior was erratic and frightening. He was a white male, isolated, and with few, if any, social or family supports. Even if the threats were never carried out, the company was already exposed to liability from the employees who had been threatened by Roger, especially because the earlier threat had been responded to inadequately. If ever there was a case to be made for terminating an employee for threatening violence, this would appear to be a prime example. And, in fact, once the reports of his statements had been substantiated, Roger could have been immediately and legitimately terminated.

What Could Have Been

Why, therefore, did the company make the right decision in not terminating Roger at once? As this case makes clear, if the company had done so, the results would likely have been disastrous for the morale and health of Roger's former work unit and ultimately troublesome for the entire company. Without doubt, the firing would have left the employees in Roger's work unit fearful, given his behavior and the threats that he had made. These employees, as well as the executives who had been involved in his firing, would be understandably fearful that Roger, potentially violent and possibly mentally unstable, would seek revenge on those responsible for his firing. But the trauma would not be limited to these individuals. Ultimately, the entire workforce would be traumatized. Rumors would spread the story, which would doubtless grow and become more scary as it was passed from mouth to mouth, department to department. And who could dispute the most frightening version? What was really known about Roger? Was he not capable of anything? Did he not fit the profile?

The Ultimate Success

Clearly, once the report was received, the company had to act. The managers could not repeat the mistake of months earlier when they essentially ignored the threat that Roger had made, failing to investigate further and failing to confront him about the reported behavior. This time, they were prepared to take action. However, to their credit, they paused and asked for help. Even more to their credit, they were willing to invest the time, the small expense, and most important, the *personal attention* to Roger that yielded such a positive result. Ultimately, the bank achieved its primary goal, which was preserving the safety and health of its employees. The fact that in the process they performed an inestimable service to Roger personally was laudable, and without doubt gratifying to these particular managers. It was, however, *the preservation of safety* that was the most important result of the process of investigation, evaluation, and counseling undertaken by the bank in response to the threats. When Roger left the bank's employ officially several months after the reports of his threatening encounter with Bill, the bank had total knowledge and confidence that he did not present a threat.

Reviewing the Employer's Actions

First Report of Threat:
Employer Agrees to Threatened Employee's
Request to Guarantee Her Anonymity

This was a dangerous and misguided decision. You cannot do that with threats of violence. You can agree to do everything possible to protect a possible target of violence, but once you have the information, you must act.

First Report of Threat:
Employer Failed to Confront
the Threatening Employee
With the Report of His Behavior

In Roger's case, the resort to the vague reference to his "behavior" in his regular review only served to confuse him because he had no idea that this was referring to the particular incident reported by Janice. As it turned out, the employer learned via the subsequent assessment that Roger was unaware of his behavior during these episodes. The employer therefore did a disservice to Roger in failing to inform him of the complaint directly and specifically. Furthermore, the bank clearly exposed itself to liability under the tort of negligent retention in its handling of this first report of threat. The indirect reference to "humorous" comments in his review was inappropriate. Presumably, the managers were making the assumption that Roger meant to be funny when he talked about bringing in his Uzi. Because they had never asked him about it, there was no basis for this assumption. In fact, the file record that documented Janice's complaint noted that Janice said that she was frightened by Roger's words because he looked serious and angry, "as though he really meant it." Given that statement, the carefully documented record of Roger's review would have been quite damaging to the bank had Roger's behavior or any actual violence had resulted in litigation or action of any kind against the employer. Finally, in essentially ignoring the seriousness of the report of Roger's behavior, the bank virtually guaranteed that additional and more serious episodes would occur. Janice's report should have served as a warning that an employee was in some kind of trouble. In fact, if Roger had gone on to commit violence, or if any subsequent dysfunctional or dangerous behavior on his part had resulted in his being hurt himself, charged with an offense, or losing his job, Roger himself could have legitimately charged the employer with negligence for failing to respond appropriately to the first report of threatening behavior.

Second Report of Threat:
Called a Consultant to Request Help

Given the apparent seriousness of the situation, the employer used good judgment in calling for outside help. This company did not have an Employee

Assistance Program or any other access to mental health or specialized medical resources. In fact, the first call was to a firm that provided outplacement services for their executives. They happened to be colleagues of ours and referred the bank directly to us. In this case, therefore, luck played a large role in getting the bank executives to the appropriate help for their situation. Therefore, although they made a good decision in asking for help, they had left themselves unprepared by not already having a plan in place. Like so many other companies, they only began the search for help in the midst of a crisis, and only luck brought them to us. As we have seen with so many of the other cases told in this book, most companies unprepared in this way are not so fortunate.

Second Report of Threat: Informed Other Employees

Here the employer demonstrated the proper application of the principle of "need to know." While the work of assessing the potential for danger went on, a second task was to deal immediately with the concerns of the employees. The bank employees were told exactly what they needed to know: that something was being done to follow up on the threat of violence, that their safety was being put first, and that they would continue to be informed. This minimized their anxiety as well as creating confidence in management. The bank's management did a good job of balancing the need to inform with the requirement to preserve Roger's privacy. This was important for two reasons. First, it protected them from any action that Roger might take in the future. Even if he were to claim that the bank had violated his privacy, defamed him, or in any other way violated his rights or hurt him, the bank would be able to show how it carefully protected his rights while doing what it had to do to protect his and others' safety. Second, the other employees witnessed firsthand how the employer acted to protect Roger's privacy and dignity throughout the process. This modeled for them how they were to act themselves, as well as showing them how they would be treated if their jobs were on the line or they had transgressed an important rule. It is impossible to overestimate how much this meant in maintaining (and possibly improving) the employer's credibility and internal reputation. This is particularly important during such a crisis, when such qualities as credibility, morale, and loyalty are very much on the line.

Summary

This case teaches us several important lessons.

The Profile Is Not a Valid or Useful Way to Prevent Workplace Violence

What if Roger had not fit the "profile"? Should the employer then have been less concerned about the threats that he had made? This case underscores the point that *behavior,* not personal characteristics, is the basis for a response to a threat. Had Roger walked around doing his job and not uttering threats but simply "fitting the profile" as he did, there would have been no reason to subject him to an investigation or take any action toward him. It was what he did, not who he was, that was important.

The Importance of the Best Information

When a threat is reported, the first concern, clearly, is safety. However, there can be no safety without information. The best safety measures are those that make information available as soon as possible. This case demonstrates this principle beautifully. If Ed and Susan had simply acted to remove Roger from the workplace, they would have at the same time removed the most important source of information. Further, the employer's careful, considerate, and thorough treatment of Roger maximized the chances of his full cooperation. Ultimately, this not only yielded a mutually satisfactory resolution of the crisis but allowed the employer to collect the highest quality information. The employer's access to the best information also allowed them to deal effectively with the employees who had been affected by Roger's disruptive and disturbing behavior.

Taking Control of the Assessment Process

The employer here, by being willing to pay for a specialized assessment outside the normal structure of health care benefits, retained control of the process and the freedom to determine exactly what kind of assessment was needed. Because the employer involved the employee at every stage of the process and maintained a personal connection with him in the crucial initial stages of the crisis, the employee felt protected rather than threatened, cared about rather than rejected.

This case, therefore, demonstrates how taking *control* is really about taking *responsibility.* Any kind of distancing, whether by a fear-driven witch hunt that focuses on a profile of characteristics or by a well-meaning banishment of the employee to an unknown specialist, translates into an abdication of responsibility and a loss of control over the process. It is up to the employer. You cannot depend on a health care specialist to bring a situation like this under control. You cannot rely on your existing human resources or disciplinary policies. You must go beyond the usual methods for resolving disputes that are in your labor relations or employee relations toolbox. All these are resources to be brought into the process, but the employer must take charge. More and more, for a growing list of crises and situations that are brought to the attention of company managers, there is a need to *respond quickly, be prepared with policies and procedures, know your resources, and use good sense and personal responsibility.* If the managers in this case had pulled back in fear or indifference and not showed real concern and commitment to Roger and their other employees, this would not have been a success story.

He's on His Way, and He's Got a Gun!

Domestic Violence Comes to the Workplace

We all remember the horrifying instance of Kitty Genovese, the young New York woman killed in the early 1960s as dozens watched and none sprang to her aid. But how many remember that when bystanders were asked later why they did not help, many responded they thought her attacker was her husband?

Mildred Pagelow, *Family Violence*

Domestic violence has come to the workplace. Today, it is the rare human resources manager or safety director who has not had to deal with this complex and frightening problem. Although not of the workplace's making, this form of violence is one that every employer must take seriously. The U.S. Department of Labor statistics tell us that homicide is *the most common cause of death for women in the workplace.* In the past decade, fully 40% of women who died at work were killed by someone (Bell et al., 1990). Clearly, it is not coworkers or unknown assailants who are responsible for these astounding statistics. The killers are almost all men who are known to the women: husbands, boyfriends, and obsessed suitors. As much as they try to protect themselves, women at work are an easy target for the harassment, stalking, and murderous violence perpetrated by these men. Of all the forms of workplace violence an employer may have to confront, *these threats have the highest risk of being carried out.*

An Office Stalking

Domestic violence overspill is a danger, not only to the safety of the employee who is being stalked or threatened, but to the physical safety and emotional health of every other employee in the work environment. Consider the example of Doris, a woman in her 20s who worked at an insurance company. Her desk sat in a large room among those of 30 other clerical employees. Her ex-boyfriend, who had several times threatened to do away with both himself and her if she persisted in her resolve to break up with him, had begun to call her at work. Doris was nervous, not only about his escalating threats and intrusion into her life, but about how this might threaten her job. Increasingly terrorized by his calls and threats to come and find her at work, she began to confide in coworkers. No one knew what to do about it. Furthermore, everyone, including the immediate supervisor, participated in uneasily "protecting" Doris from what might happen if the office manager found out about these phone calls. One day, slamming down the phone and bolting up from her chair, Doris screamed, "He's coming here, and he's got a gun!" Shortly after this incident, the employer did indeed take action. Sadly, I learned about this case, not as a consultant engaged by the company to help find a solution to an existing problem, but from reading the decision of a labor arbitrator after Doris sued to get her job back.

This is an example of a crisis that could have been prevented. Doris was fired because the threats from her boyfriend were disrupting the workplace and causing a safety hazard. On the face of it, this was certainly true, and the arbitrator in fact did uphold the termination. But was this a successful resolution of this crisis? Whose responsibility was it to see that this hazard was brought to the attention of the workplace as soon as the first threat was made? If the boyfriend had come to the office and hurt Doris or others in the process, who would have been at fault for failing to protect employees from a known hazard? Who can calculate the costs to the employer of the months of fear and discomfort suffered by this work group because of this man's terrorizing?

The failure to adopt policies to ensure early notification of threats sets the stage for disasters and disputes. It also allows the serious disruption of the productivity and health of the affected employee to remained undetected and unchecked. Doris could not have been expected to function adequately at work while living with the constant fear of harassment and threats from a stalker. As a matter of policy, management should have been informed *as soon as there was the first sign or warning* of a workplace stalking situation.

Helpless Managers

In fact, can there be any doubt that someone in a management or supervisory position was aware, to some extent, about the situation in Doris' work group? Managers often do know about these things, but the sad fact is that they do not know what to do about them. In the absence of company policies, and increasingly in these times of downsizing, first-line and middle managers keep these messy situations to themselves: "If I bother the boss about this, he'll think I can't handle my area. Besides, he won't know how to handle it either. Maybe if I ignore it, it will go away. Maybe I can try to help—we'll offer her counseling. . . ." A post office case from several years ago offers a chilling and saddening example of this. Although it happened at a small, rural post office, these situations happen everywhere in the USA, in white-, blue-, and grey-collar environments.

As the postmaster in a town of 8,000 perched near a mountain pass high in the Rockies, June supervised three postal clerks and oversaw the activities of five letter carriers. She was particularly close to Mary, a clerk who had been there for June's entire tenure as manager. It was natural for Mary to come to June when the threats and harassment from Mary's ex-husband escalated to promises that he would kill her. The internal security report issued 9 months later chronicled 21 separate acts that June took over the 8-month period between the time that Mary first informed her of the threats and the day that her ex-husband killed her, at her home, in the presence of their children. These acts included granting Mary time off to obtain restraining orders from the court, helping her seek out counseling help, looking for shelters, and pursuing restraining orders and criminal charges with the local police. June stayed very busy trying to help her employee and trying to protect her workplace from the threat.

Only one act was omitted from June's list: *She never went to her higher-ups in the Postal Service to inform them about the threats.* June, as the sole manager of this small government agency outpost, chose to handle this highly hazardous situation herself. Even though it had a high probability of harm to the employee as well as to the entire workplace, June did not inform her boss or the postal internal security service that this situation existed. One might explain this by simply saying, "This woman lacked judgment and fundamental common sense. She was well-meaning but clearly incompetent when it came to handling threats of violence. A better manager would have known what to do." But this appeal to common sense makes the argument for the need for clear policies to direct the actions of managers in cases of domestic violence threats. As an employer, you do not want to depend on the judgment of individual managers in the handling of threats. June had never been provided with any training or specific policy direction on how to handle this kind of situation.

Policies exist, not only to ensure timely response to threats, but to support managers and protect employees from unnecessary stress. June may not have been able to prevent Mary's death. But what about the toll on June's health and productivity over those 8 months? What about the residual effects on her health and job longevity in the aftermath of this horror? What about the risk to the workplace that existed for the entire period that Mary continued to report for work under the shadow of the threats?

Principles of Domestic Violence Prevention

Everything we have learned so far about the principles for prevention of workplace violence applies to domestic violence overspill, including early warning, coordinated response, and close involvement from top management levels. Observe these three guides when formulating your company domestic violence policies:

Rule Number 1: Encourage reliable and early warning. The key to early warning is the report of the threatened employee herself. There are powerful forces that will mitigate against your employee's telling you that she is or may be the victim of domestic violence or stalking. In the absence of powerful, clear, and well-supported policies on your part, she (or he) will make one or more *assumptions* about informing you of the situation. These assumptions are: (a) As my employer, you do not want to know about it; it is my personal problem, and "none of your business;" and (b) Disclosing to you that I am the victim of domestic violence will threaten my employment. To counteract these assumptions you must communicate to your employees that domestic threat *is* your business. It is very much "your business" because it affects the health and productivity of the employee who is the victim and because it presents a potential risk to the entire workplace. Rather than being concerned about the negative consequences of disclosing the situation to you, your employees should fear your reaction if they *do not* inform you as soon as possible that a threat has been made or that a situation is developing. In addition, they need the same assurances of confidentiality and nonretaliation that apply to the policy that covers internal sexual harassment.

Rule Number 2: Ensure manager involvement. Ensure that once your management staff become aware of a possible risk, they communicate it to the proper levels immediately. In the face of such a risk, you don't want to rely on common sense or ask managers to make judgment calls! As the head of a company or agency, you want to know that these situations will be handled precisely the way you have decided they should be handled. Train your managers well about this. Make sure that they know that failure to inform will be considered a performance issue.

Rule Number 3: Take team action. Whether you are the office manager, the human resources director, or the head of security, *don't ever try to handle a domestic violence situation alone.* Domestic overspill and stalkings are scary, complex, and frustrating to confront. They raise complicated questions, and the risks of violence are among the highest you will ever face. Assemble a team as soon as you become aware of a situation so that you can gather information, consult together, and make decisions as a group.

Rule Number 4: Know the law. Integrate knowledge of federal and state laws and familiarity with local procedures and resources into your policy. Know how you can be involved directly in enforcing a restraining order and how you can work with local law enforcement. Some companies have made it a matter of company policy to obtain an order restraining anyone who threatens an employee from approaching, entering, or contacting the workplace. Too often, feeling overwhelmed by the prospect of involvement with these confusing and frightening matters, employers wash their hands. Though this is understandable, it is a foolhardy approach given the relatively high risk represented by this class of workplace violence. The only way to overcome the position of helplessness is to take the issue on directly and aggressively. Like it or not, the employer is a primary player when a domestic violence threat touches the workplace.

An example of this kind of active stance is the effect of the 1996 domestic violence gun ban on police departments. This federal law prohibits gun ownership or possession by anyone ever convicted of a domestic violence offense of any degree. Increasing numbers of police departments, realizing the implications of this law for their officers, are using it as an opportunity to respond to the shockingly high levels of domestic violence found among police officers. The inability to carry a weapon prevents a police officer from performing normal peace officer duties and usually results in dismissal or restriction to a desk assignment. The enactment of this law has gone far to counteract the institutionalized denial of the problem that has existed in law enforcement. Many departments have followed up with training, education, and other measures to prevent domestic violence in their ranks. Other industries should follow this example in confronting all forms of denial of the ways in which domestic violence affects the well-being and safety of the workforce.

Summary (a Footnote)

As I was completing this chapter, I received a call from a newspaper reporter who was writing a story about domestic violence and the workplace. The story had been prompted by a incident in his city in which a husband, who worked with his wife in the same factory, had ambushed her outside the facility as she arrived for their shift. Killing her with a shotgun, he then turned the weapon on himself. The husband had been arrested 6 months previously for threatening and beating his wife but had avoided prosecution by completing a 2-month batterers' education program that was offered in conjunction with the court. The reporter had several questions for me, including: What did I think of these court diversion programs? (The local people, outraged at the crime, were asking themselves the same thing.) He also wanted to know, given that the employer had not known about the husband's arrest for battering, what I thought about the situation where a batterer and his victim worked in the same place. My response to his questions was to ask why the company *didn't know* that the husband had been arrested for domestic violence. I used this question as a springboard for my comments to him about the importance of a proactive, highly visible, and well-enforced internal workplace policy on domestic violence.

As the reporter and I spoke about the limitations of judicial and law enforcement responses to this fierce, frightening crime and the complications and challenges of dealing with situations of this kind when they involve the employment setting, I found myself saying to the reporter, "It's easy to shoot holes in the solutions of individual players in these scenarios." Yes, the law can be gotten around. Yes, companies drop the ball by closing their eyes or passing the buck. But the nature of this crime is that any perpetrator can and will try to push through legal or policy barriers to his harassing and violent acts. Given that, the only hope is communication, teamwork, and diligent, persistent, and patient collaboration among an alliance of stakeholders. The company in this case needed to have awareness of this situation as early as possible so that it could begin to decide how to handle it with everyone's safety in mind. Beyond that, however, it would have been an absolute requirement to create a close tie with local law enforcement and the court handling the case. Only then would there be a chance of acting to preserve the safety of the employee and the workplace at large.

Confronting cases of domestic violence is a scary, complex, and frustrating process. Because of this, the greatest barrier to prevention is the tendency to deny or avoid. As an employer, it is easy to do that by passing the responsibility on to the courts or other public entities. The employer, however, does that at its peril. After enacting its own ironclad internal policy, therefore, the next essential step is to ensure that any actions of the employer are fully coordinated with those of other public and community entities.

The Legal Conundrum:

What Is the Employer's Duty?

After a certain level of the problem has been reached, legalistic thinking
induces paralysis; it prevents one from seeing the scale and
meaning of events.

Alexander Solzhenitsyn, *A World Split Apart*

One common reason for the mishandling of threat of violence cases is the advice that employers get from their lawyers. This is not to say that lawyers have no sense or that they do not base their advice on sound legal principles. The reason lies in the history of employment in America and the way that those laws have shaped our approaches to employee safety and rights.

Our culture elevates independence and the protection of property as essential rights of the individual. In the employment arena, these values are expressed in laws designed to protect employees against the employer's use of personal information to withhold compensation or deny or terminate employment. Indeed, a plethora of laws to protect the rights of the employee against possible abuse by employers have grown up because of our system of "employment at will." Because most employment law is founded on the protection of these rights, employment attorneys approach violence and threat situations with these principles foremost in their minds. Unfortunately, these principles, although valid, are in conflict with an equally compelling and equally valid set of legal principles that bear directly on violence and threats in the workplace. These are known as the duty to provide a safe workplace, or "due diligence," or, in the United States, "duty of care." The challenge for companies and their attorneys is to balance these often conflicting principles.

A Zealous Corporate Attorney

Recently, I had an interaction with an attorney that illustrates this point. It resembles scores of such conversations I have had over the years. A power company contacted me about a reported threat from an employee who was on an injury leave. This lineman had been away from the job on numerous extended medical leaves since he had been seriously injured when a utility pole fell on him 8 years previously. For the past 2 years, he had been suing the company to keep him on workers' compensation and was now claiming that his disabilities were the result of the psychological stress caused by this accident. The company claimed that because the claim for psychological stress was new and the 2-year "statute of limitations" had expired for a claim of emotional stress, and because he had refused to undergo recommended surgery on his back, the law did not require the company to compensate him any further. For 2 years, the employee, a divorced man in his 40s, now on his second lawyer, had pursued litigation to reverse that decision, punctuated only by several hospitalizations for depression and treatments for the proliferation of musculoskeletal conditions linked to the accident. The power company's lawyers, feeling that the law was on their side, refused to consider a lump sum settlement that had been proposed by the employee's lawyer. They figured that a waiting game with an employee who was not getting paid was the best strategy. That strategy was about to backfire.

On the day I was called, the company's head of security had just been informed that the employee had told his attorney that he was going to take his gun and kill the people from the insurance company that was denying his claim, and that, while he was at it, he would take care of the people at the power company as well. I was asked to evaluate the situation with respect to this man's dangerousness and to recommend a plan of action.

My conversation with the company lawyer (we'll call him Bob) occurred when I asked to see the personnel file of the employee, which included medical records and reports of medical and psychological evaluations. "That's protected information," Bob informed me. "I can't let you see it without a release from the employee." Bob was doing his job: Following time-honored and precedent-based employee law, he was protecting the company against the possibility of being sued for violating the employee's privacy. I pointed out to Bob that although I understood the law and respected the need to protect the employee's privacy, this was a situation where we had to evaluate whether a risk of violence existed. In my role as an expert, I needed access to the information contained in the employee's record to help the company decide what steps might be necessary to protect the safety of its employees. Providing a safe workplace, I reminded Bob, was also a matter of law: The duty to provide a safe workplace required that an employer protect employees from a possible threat to health or safety. Having been made aware of a possible threat, the company was now required to take steps commensurate with the level of threat. Was Bob aware, I asked, of the threatening statements that the employee was reported to have made? Was he prepared to take responsibility for someone's being harmed because we had felt constrained from taking prompt and appropriate action?

The Rock and the Hard Place: Conflicting Legal Principles

If Bob was put into a dilemma by my words, that is not surprising. There was, clearly, a conflict here between the laws protecting privacy and those that require an employer to protect the safety of employees while at work. Bob, like every other employment lawyer I had ever encountered, whether working for companies or representing employees, had been schooled thoroughly in one set of those laws, those concerning employee rights. This is because most of the employment law that has been practiced in this country has involved the litigation of suits in which employees claim violation of their rights by the employer. Usually, the "right" involves violation of privacy, discrimination, or another alleged unfair practice. Attorneys working for corporations see it as their job to advise their clients against actions that might expose them to these lawsuits. It is a defensive posture, usually producing advice to *avoid* some action. As in our present example, this advice often reflects a narrow, rigid view of the situation: *Don't* arrange to have your employee put under surveillance (even though he left the workplace in a rage yesterday, threatening to return to exact payback, and his wife hasn't seen him since he came home to get his rifle). *Don't* make a call to the physician who has been treating your employee to inquire about possible homicidality (even though his supervisor and coworkers report that he has been slipping into a suicidal despair for weeks, is on final warning, and is the suspected author of a threatening letter to the CEO).

Bob's action was a good example of the dangers of the defensive position. While the impaired employee remains isolated, his condition possibly worsening, the employer sits, similarly isolated, deprived of the tools he or she needs to evaluate the situation and take action.

The traditional legal posture protects against one sort of legal exposure but fails to consider other, potentially much more serious risks. When the two legal principles are in conflict, it is not a question of weighing the validity or value of one principle against another, for both are useful and important. What is dangerous is to apply one principle and ignore the other. These situations require that employers not think in black and white terms. To make sound decisions in confronting threats, it is necessary is to understand the principles underlying the laws and then to find a balance based on an assessment of the relative risks. To return, then, to the case of the zealous corporate counsel, this is how I addressed this issue with him:

> Bob, I understand that you want to avoid a violation of privacy here, and the law about that is clear. But the law is also clear about the duty to preserve safety, and we have to weigh the relative risks here. Let me ask you this: Suppose this employee were to carry out his threats. Which lawsuit would you rather be defending: his claim that you unlawfully released his records, or that of the family of a dead or injured coworker claiming that you did not protect their husband or son despite having been warned of the danger? Even if no actual violence occurs, you need to consider that you already have a number of employees who are quite frightened about these reports of possible violence. They could claim that you did not act to protect them and that they have suffered stress as a result. You should be aware that security has already made a decision to put this employee under surveillance for the next 72 hours pending further information and the results of my and others' investigations.

At that, Bob began to yield, and we agreed on a limited release of those records that I judged to be relevant to my investigation at that point. Bob was smart enough to realize that even if no violence ever ensued, he would be able to defend his decision to release the records in the event of possible legal action by an employee (or former employee) or questioning by superiors.

A Map for the Minefield

Good crisis management requires judgment calls. The decisions facing you are rarely clear cut. Conflicting legal, ethical, and security issues mean that you have to consider the risks and drawbacks of any action, make your best call, and document the decision-making process so that you are prepared to defend it if necessary. You do not need to have made the "right" decision to be able to defend yourself; you simply have to show that you responsibly and diligently collected information, consulted adequately with the proper people, and, establishing your own rationale, made a decision. The best defense, therefore, is not inaction or the withholding of information. It is the documentation of a good process.

It is more and more important to have systems in place to ensure that you will be able to handle these crises successfully. The requirements of the Americans with Disabilities Act, state and federal antidiscrimination statutes, and the complexities of employment law create a minefield of confusing and potentially conflicting decisions for the human resources director, risk manager, or company executive. To be sure, the risks of being sued for discrimination or invasion of privacy under the protection of these federal or state statutes are very real. Lawsuits based on these statutes, even if they are frivolous or far-fetched and have little chance of success, are costly to companies. Therefore, it is understandable that companies have become extremely concerned about avoiding such suits.

The advice to employers about this can and does approach the absurd. A recent national publication on employment issues, citing the recent addition of mental health to the Americans with Disabilities Act, related the case of a terminated employee who had sued his employer. The employee had been fired for poor performance, but he claimed that he had been unfairly terminated because an emotional disability had interfered with his ability to perform adequately. The basis of his suit was that the employer had offered him the services of the Employee Assistance Program (EAP). This was true: Early in the progressive discipline process, the employer had made this suggestion with the thought that family stresses might be playing a role in his missing work and making errors. The employee now claimed that this meant that the employer had identified that an emotional disability that contributed to his performance problems. As such, the argument went, the employer had violated the ADA by firing him. The author of the article, citing this case, advised employers that because mental disability was now specifically included as a protected disability, employers should refrain from recommending the EAP to employees who were having job performance problems!

I recounted this case recently to a hospital management team who came to me with the case of a nurse who had made veiled threats about her gun collection when she was suspended for physically abusing a patient. They had considered a psychiatric assessment but were advised by their lawyer not to do this because in so doing they would run afoul of the Americans with Disabilities Act. Instead, they were considering transferring her to a less stressful unit and referring her to the EAP. I pointed out that this action would violate their violence policy by not responding directly to the veiled threat and, more important, would leave them in the dark about her possible dangerousness. Furthermore, the counseling referral, besides being inappropriate as the response to a possible threat, would still create the risk of a discrimination claim. I recommended that a specialized dangerousness assessment was precisely what they needed and that any decisions about job continuation or placement should be deferred pending the results. In the case of a claim of discrimination, I assured them, they could justify their requirement for an assessment on the basis of their duty to provide a safe workplace. They could further point out that they had made no assumptions about a mental health condition in taking this action and that they were not asking for a mental health evaluation at all—the process was solely directed toward an assessment of dangerousness. The team saw the sense of this and agreed to proceed in this way.

The Duty of Care

Bob's advice and the counsel of the hospital's lawyer are both examples of how attorneys' efforts to protect employers from possible lawsuits can have the effect of exposing the employer to a far greater risk. In both cases, following the advice would have caused the employer to neglect its duty of care under U.S. law. In practical terms, the duty of care consists of two components: (a) the federal law under the federal Occupational Safety and Health Act of 1971 (OSHA) and (b) principles of civil law.

Federal Law

OSHA requires that an employer provide a safe workplace. Under the general duty clause, the act states that the employer is responsible for any condition that represents a hazard to the life, safety, or psychological well-being of employees at the workplace. An employer is responsible for injuries or illness resulting from conditions in the workplace, including violence, threats of physical harm, and the creation of a hostile work environment. Under this law, employers are negligent if they fail to recognize a potential hazard and take steps to correct the condition. They have broken the law if they allow such behavior by employees or create a risk through their management practices.

Civil Law

Negligent Hiring

Employers are liable if they fail to show reasonable diligence in ensuring that an employee would not present a danger to others while he or she is on the job. This negligence can occur in at least two ways. The first involves the nature of the work. For example, if the job involves access to property or dwellings, such as that of a caretaker, an employer would have to exercise care in ensuring that the person did not have a history of assault. In one case, the management of an apartment complex hired a caretaker who had been convicted of forcible entry to commit rape. When the man used his key to enter an apartment and sexually assault a woman, the employer was held liable for negligent hiring. The second involves ignoring or failing to consider information that would indicate an obvious risk. In a well-known case, a company that had fired a man for stalking and threatening a female employee rehired him years later. He went on to stalk and kill a female employee that he met during this second tenure at the company. Knowledge of this law is important when employers try to observe the numerous laws prohibiting asking certain questions on hiring. It is important, in other words, to know when it is allowed, even required, to elevate safety over privacy. The laws protecting prospective hires from discrimination must be balanced against this aspect of the duty of care.

Negligent Retention

A company is liable under the law of negligent retention if it fails to take action with respect to an employee who may threaten or pose a risk of harm to fellow employees, customers or clients, or members of the public who enter or have contact with the workplace. As soon as employers gain information that would lead to suspicion or belief that anyone is put at risk by their employee, they are obligated to investigate and to take corrective action. Failure to take immediate action when there is evidence that the employee is the cause of injury, illness, or the creation of a hostile and thus unhealthy and unsafe working environment exposes the employer to liability if claims are brought by individuals alleging that they or family members have been harmed. As an employer, you can diligently pursue these actions when a danger or possible danger has been brought to your attention *without* illegally compromising the rights of your employees if you exercise good sense and an understanding of the principles that underlie the laws.

Negligent Supervision

If its employees are acting in an inappropriate, unprofessional, or harmful manner, the company is negligent if it does not correct this condition. According to U.S. law, a company is responsible for the consequences of the behavior of its managers in the performance of their duties. An employer must evaluate the performance of its employees, including its management staff, with respect to their treatment of their employees and their adherence to standards of behavior dictated by company policy and law. It is not enough to evaluate managers simply according to their productivity.

How Is It Done?

How, then, can company management continue to respect the laws protecting privacy and "protected groups" while still responding diligently to any risk of violence? Here again, we return to the importance of a good process. If you are mindful of the principles underlying the laws, you can act in ways that mitigate the drawbacks of whatever action you choose. Here are some guidelines.

Remember That the Privacy of Medical Records Can Be Waived

Most employers, intimidated by the issue of privacy and skittish about dealing directly with health care professionals, have forgotten or ignored this obvious option. If you want the records opened, or if you want to talk to a psychiatrist or therapist who has treated the employee, *ask the employee for permission.* If you have acted wisely by involving the employee early on in your investigation, your employee will agree and will grant this permission. Usually, employees do this willingly, even eagerly, because they are eager to clear their name and are relieved that the employer cares enough to want to talk to the doctor. Only after you have requested this waiver and it has been denied, or, as in our present case, circumstances make it impossible or impractical to obtain it, may you decide to act unilaterally to gain access to protected information.

Establish Limits to the Information
That You Acquire

Assure your employee that *only* the information that you need will be obtained from his doctor. In the case of a threat of violence, you are asking for an opinion about his safety in the workplace. As the employer, you require only information that helps answer that question. Details of current personal life, history, or psychiatric or medical diagnoses *may* be relevant to the question, but if they are not, you do not want them! Be sure that you are clear with the doctor about this as well.

Observe the "Need to Know"

Restrict and monitor the information flow. If you open up records or obtain medical information from an outside source, share what you find only with the consultant whose opinion you are requesting, and only with management personnel who are required to participate in the decision-making process. If you are interviewing other employees, tell them only what you absolutely must to learn what you need to learn from them. Tell them that you must be careful in what you share to protect the privacy of the individual in question, and enjoin them to do the same by not talking to anyone else about this. Document the reason for any sharing of information with employees or other third parties.

Follow the Principles and Goals
Underlying the Laws

Finally, dealing with threats and violence requires that the employer go beyond adherence to the letter of the law. As we have seen, the laws pertaining to violence or threat often appear to be in conflict with one another. When these apparent conflicts arise, it becomes essential to understand and apply the laws at a principled level. Good crisis management practice requires sound judgment, teamwork, reasoned decision making, collaborative information gathering, and compassion. Knowledge of the law alone will not guarantee that these qualities are present when dealing with a threat from an impaired employee or a worker who claims that he has been traumatized by an assault. Rather, like that elusive commodity called common sense, effective violence prevention and crisis management require the application of two core values and principles: safety and respect for the individual.

Safety

It should go without saying, but experience shows us that this simple fact must be continually reinforced: The purpose of violence prevention procedures and policies is to protect people from harm. Many of the cases described in this book are examples of how safety has been ignored or compromised because people, even when faced with a clear danger, did not look beyond the rules. Other issues, such as the protection of privacy or adherence to the letter of a collective bargaining agreement, must be considered, but only after safety is ensured.

Respect for the Individual

The law provides a foundation for the protection of rights to privacy and dignity. However, employers who rely on the law alone to ensure their employees' rights are protected and that their employees are treated fairly do so at their peril. As several of our cases demonstrate, simple reliance on legal advice or standard procedures for discipline or health management is often a prescription for disaster. The very nature of crisis practically guarantees that "following procedure" will allow incipient crises to brew rather than to get the special attention they deserve. At worst—and not uncommonly—procedures that have been designed for a situation far removed from a threat or a risk of violence actually add to the problem and accelerate or even cause the conflict or violence-related crisis. When violence and employees' sense of security and trust are at issue, only people acting planfully and consciously can safeguard rights and ensure the preservation of individual dignity and organizational health.

10

Workplace Violence and Labor Relations:

From Battleground to Collaboration

> *The positive benefits of conflict include the airing of problems that an*
> *employer needs to address and the resulting beneficial changes in*
> *such areas as policies, programs, organizational structure, and*
> *productivity. It can be a constructive force for innovation.*
> Sandra Gleason, *Workplace Dispute Resolution*

A Consultant Is Tarred With His Own Brush

In 1995, I organized a symposium on workplace violence for the annual meeting of the American Public Health Association (APHA). Unaware of APHA's strong roots in the labor movement, I was surprised to find myself speaking not only to employers and occupational health professionals but to a number of people from unions, who had come because they had strong feelings about the issue. Among the speakers I had invited was an attorney from a law firm that represents employers in employment disputes. In my talk, I advocated a public health-style prevention approach to the workplace violence issue. The attorney focused on how employers could shield themselves from being sued by employees who were exposed to violence from other workers and how to identify the worker who might become violent. This orientation angered the union people. Before long, we were being—to put it delicately—aggressively challenged by a significant portion of the audience. Their argument went like this:

> This workplace violence issue is another way for employers to punish deviant or activist employees and to find scapegoats for other safety problems. Even though the data say that only 4% of the violence is worker on worker, it is always the "violent employee" that is the focus of these presentations! We want to see the employer take responsibility for the real problem, which is that our members are being injured and murdered by people from outside the workplace and assaulted by clients or patients. Clearly, employers don't care about these real exposures. You and your lawyer friend have developed a nice cottage industry here. You are exploiting the fears and selfishness of employers, and you are doing it by blaming the victim.

Who Is Defining the Problem?

I was upset and embarrassed because I should have known better. The union people were correct: The National Institute of Occupational Safety and Health had recently identified violence originating from nonemployees, chiefly through armed robbery and assault by clients and patients, as the leading cause of violence-related fatalities and nonfatal injuries at work. Several unions, notably those that represent service workers, had begun to focus on this problem.[1] Their position was: "The union will confront the employer for failing to recognize this hazard. We will work to ensure that programs are adopted to ameliorate it." This is a time-honored and valid position for a union to take. But in this position lies the very problem confronting us if we really want to tackle workplace violence: The issue has become *adversarial.* As such, it becomes polarized, and the available facts are liable to misinterpretation. Saying that worker-on-worker violence is a negligible part of the problem is a distortion based on a misreading of the existing data. The statistic that only 4% of workplace violence is between employees is based on U.S. Department of Labor data for *fatalities only.* It does not reflect the reality of worker-on-worker violence in all of its forms, including nonfatal assaults, fights, and threats. We do not have statistics for these beyond what we can estimate from surveys. I believe on the basis of my own experience and several surveys that it is a significant problem. But the unions want to say, "Worker-on-worker violence is not a big problem; it is being used to avoid responsibility for doing what needs to be done to fix the real threats to employee safety."

Trading on Quick Fixes

At the same time, their criticism is valid: An opportunistic industry of consultants and attorneys *has* grown up around this issue. Aided by the media, these law firms, consulting groups, trainers, and publishers are trading on the sensationalistic picture of the homicidal paranoid, bent on revenge, who must be identified and stopped. They are exploiting the fear and the ever-present hunger for quick solutions and easy targets for blame by offering a range of training, educational, and evaluation tools. These products purport to "protect" the employer from the threat of violent employees. Although these products and approaches may contain useful information, they are of limited usefulness and may be actually dangerous because the employer, having bought the video or the handbook, feels that he has now taken care of the problem. But he has not: What he *has* bought is an inaccurate, narrow view of the problem, and he has neglected several crucial steps.

First, he has not involved employees by asking them about their own experience with violence at work. Second, he has not created a stakeholder alliance by involving unions and other critical constituents in the assessment and planning stages. Without these steps, there is little chance that any of the employer's efforts will amount to anything. Furthermore, by focusing on "the enemy within," the employer risks frightening and alienating his workforce, creating overreactions and witch hunts, and demoralizing workers who may be at risk for other types of violence. Those employees will continue to believe that there is no help or caring forthcoming, and they will indeed feel mistrusted and blamed. By "buying" this narrow view of workplace violence, the employer has missed an opportunity to forge a coalition around a new problem that needs an entirely new set of solutions.

Reframing Workplace Health and Safety Policy

Agreeing to Agree

Look at the degree of conflict and controversy that surrounds this topic, and you realize the enormous meaning it carries with respect to the employment relationship. To focus this issue, let us imagine a roundtable of corporate and union leaders, and let us put them on the spot. Let us turn to the employer first and ask, "Are you interested in protecting yourself from your employees or in forging an alliance with them to address a common problem?" While he or she considers this question, let us ask the union official, "Are you preparing for yet another battle to keep management honest, or are you interested in forging a coalition with management and other stakeholders to reduce a threat to the safety of everyone in the workplace?"

My uncomfortable experience at the conference was not important. Of devastating import, however, is how this battle is being waged every day in our office buildings and factories. It is crucial that we reframe the controversy about violence in the workplace. The adversarial process designed to resolve labor disputes, based on negotiation and compromise and involving the stepwise grievance-to-arbitration process, is totally inappropriate as an approach to issues involving threat, intimidation, or dangerous behavior. This is about protecting workers from possible or imminent harm, not about resolving disputes about pay, job security, work rules, or other issues that might be part of a labor agreement. The first step is for the stakeholders to agree that the problem requires a new approach. The paradox is that to know where to begin, they need not look further than the standard, time-honored topics of safety and health.

Safety

Workplace safety as a field needs to be redefined and broadened to reflect new complexities and new hazards. Violence must be added to the growing list of environmental hazards that may affect people at work. *Traditional approaches to safety are not adequate to address the hazard of violence.* Under the existing, traditional approach, unions and management each embrace different components of the violence problem. On the labor side, unions advocate for work rules, environmental design, and security procedures to protect workers from assault from nonemployees. However, protection from assaults from outside the workplace does not address the fear of threats from fellow employees, which is a real concern in many workplaces. Furthermore, such programs are useless without real employer commitment. On the employer side, employers push for tighter pre-employment screening and tough policies for potential offenders within the workforce. Again, these may be useful steps, but they are ineffective and potentially divisive if not founded on an effective alliance with employees and well-designed systems for true crisis response that provide a sense of security for workers. They will backfire when accompanied by the apparent denial of the reality of nonemployee sources of violence such as armed robbery, domestic violence overspill, or assaults from patients.

Health

Confronting workplace violence reveals the need to revisit and modify existing systems of occupational health care and disability policy. It also requires that employers change the way disciplinary policy is applied to the following behavioral and occupational health issues:

Preventive Health Care for Violence-Related Injuries

Employees at risk for traumatic stress reactions because of exposure to violence and threat require preventive mental health care. This may be in the form of training for at-risk employee groups (primary prevention), counseling and education for employees at the point of injury or exposure (secondary prevention), and specialized treatment for employees exhibiting stress-related problems in the aftermath of exposures (tertiary prevention). *Preventive care related to these exposures will not happen within established delivery and coverage systems.* The provision of occupational health services in virtually all of today's health care environments—whether publicly or privately administered—is based on cost containment (e.g., restricted access, control over utilization, and distancing of the employer from the administration of care) rather than prevention. Preventive intervention in the form of education, assessment, and counseling before a claim has occurred is not part of such systems. This means that any effective program for preventive care of violence-related injuries must function outside these systems. The care should be employer managed and employer financed. Responsibility for such programming must originate at a corporate policy level. In a unionized workplace, management should invite labor to participate in this process. This may be done through established structures such as safety committees or through the establishment of innovative collaborations, such as site-based joint crisis or violence prevention teams.

Assessment of Employees at Risk for or Suspected of Violent Behavior

An employee about whom such concerns are raised may be facing a health issue. However, this is not always the case: It is as much a mistake to automatically send the employee suspected of dangerousness for a psychological evaluation as it is to immediately fire him or take legal action against him (Chapter 11 takes up this issue in detail). In many cases, however, an evaluation is required to assess the risk of violence and reach an understanding of the causes for the problematic behavior. Here, too, most existing systems designed to establish psychological fitness for work are not adequate or appropriate when the question concerns dangerousness. A referral through the established health delivery network is not likely to yield an adequate assessment. Even if the professional has the needed skills, he or she will not be able to apply them under the constraints of the health care system (an office visit is not a system-level dangerousness assessment). Furthermore, as long as standard disciplinary procedures are in effect, the assessment will be performed under a cloud of the threat of punishment. This mitigates powerfully against valid information collection and smooth coordination of response. Labor will be forced to respond to the discipline through the grievance-arbitration procedure, which thwarts accurate, collaborative, and neutral information gathering. Again, this is where the employer, in an alliance with labor, health care providers, and other constituents, must take responsibility for creating the systems and identifying the resources needed to perform these functions. Assessment of the behavioral and health issues will not happen and will not be usefully applied unless it is guided by strong leadership and proactive planning.

The Challenge

The fear of violence is felt in all quarters. It is felt by CEOs who are struggling, perhaps unconsciously, with their sense of the fear, desperation, and rage that exist all around them. It is felt by union presidents who experience a similar loss of control over their mandate to represent and protect, as well as feeling deeply the desperation, loss, and pain experienced by their membership. The need for new systems and a renewed spirit of collaboration will continue to grow. We can expect an increase in the frequency of incidents involving individual breakdown and threat because of the increasing economic pressure on families and the removal of societal supports in the form of health care and other services. We can expect an increase in conflict and incidents at work because of increased work pressure. This will undoubtedly be true for supervisory and management personnel as well as line workers. Supervisors in particular are caught in the vise of doing more with less and are at risk for their job security as well. As a result, they must drive their workers harder and may feel that they cannot "afford" to attend to the human needs of their workers or to pay much attention to their communication and management skills.

Unions face their own challenges. Members in traditionally "protected" industries such as government and utilities now face downsizing. Collective bargaining is of limited, if any, use in protecting members' job security in the face of these developments. These challenges are not limited to particular industries, however. Employers and unions across the globe are recognizing the need for new approaches to new realities. As a current writer (Gleason, 1997) observed, "Employers around the world are seeking ways to effectively handle disputes arising over the changes in employment practices required to survive in an increasingly global economy" (p. 3). As economic and job performance pressure mounts, unions find themselves in the position of having to handle an increasing load of unhappiness and distress among their constituents. In some workplaces, where labor-management collaboration is low and there may be no Employee Assistance Program (EAP), or where the EAP enjoys little confidence, unions are acting as the de facto counseling and drug counseling service. In more and more cases, unions are actually on the front line in defusing dangerous threat situations as well as suicide crises. I have sat with officials of the United Mine Workers who tell me in confidence that they are handling cases of assault, threat, and suicide risk on a weekly basis, shielding these cases from management and from standard disciplinary and safety procedures. These highly committed union officers told me that they knew that they were playing with fire but that under the current labor-management conditions, they had no choice. They said that they would jump at the chance to sit at a table with the company and talk about how to collaboratively deal with these common problems. Never have unions been more motivated to find ways to work with the employer to defuse conflict and decrease the frequency of threatening and violent incidents.

The search for solutions requires a nonadversarial approach to labor-management relations. Any workplace that is serious about protecting employees from violence or from the fear of violence must take a good look at what kind of relationship prevails between management and employees. If there is a union, it is an opportunity to look for ways to truly join in the planning and implementation of a prevention program. I have seen this happen in postal districts where union and management have joined to craft violence prevention policies that depart from established labor relations procedures. Using joint teams for information gathering and consensus, they have brought grievances down sharply, made discipline more rare and more effective, improved morale, and reduced dramatically the costs associated with labor disputes, stress claims, and disability cases.

Management as well needs to find new ways to promote collaboration with unions. When conflict between supervisors and employees is handled strictly through labor relations channels, all parties are prevented from looking for real solutions to critical human needs. For example, managers may be in dire need of seminars to help them relieve their own stress or for training to improve their management skills. Employees may be feeling needs for a stronger voice in the organization of their work, greater flexibility in work schedules, or changes in working conditions. In a negative labor relations environment, individual voices are seldom heard, and changes come late, grudgingly, or not at all as the adversarial process grinds along. Increasingly, employers as well as unions are seeking alternative methods to resolve disputes as the costs of these dysfunctional systems become clearer:

> There is widespread discontent with the costs and delays of grievance procedures, arbitration, and litigated settlements. Less costly and faster alternatives with more satisfactory outcomes are being sought. This search for better methods has encouraged some employers to experiment with preventive approaches to empower employees to self-manage disputes, including a variety of forms of labor-management cooperative activities, and integrated conflict management systems. (Gleason, 1997, p. 7)

Companies can no longer afford the luxury of tolerating the waste and danger of adversarial labor relations. The violence issue provides an opportunity to move decisively into a future of collaboration and innovation. Leaders in industry and labor alike must have the vision and courage to recognize and seize this opportunity.

Note

1. Jordan Barab, the assistant director of health and safety for AFSCME, the union that represents many public sector and service industry employees, is an eloquent spokesman for a progressive labor perspective on the violence issue. AFSCME's national office in Washington, D.C., is a good source of materials and information on the topic.

11

Assessing the Risk of Violence:

Know Your Questions!

Only a free man can negotiate; prisoners cannot enter into contracts.
Nelson Mandela, statement from prison, 1985

When there is a report of a threat, or someone raises a concern about violence, the employer faces a crisis, *whether or not an actual risk of violence exists.* Like any report of a safety risk, it requires immediate attention. Like any incident involving possible misconduct, such as a report of sexual harassment, it requires great care in the conduct of an investigation because it involves people's right to privacy. Slip-ups and fumbles can be damaging and costly to individuals and to the company as a whole. Yet as we saw in a number of our cases, employers regularly commit serious errors in the way that they attempt to answer the central questions: Is this employee dangerous? And if so, under what circumstances?

In fact, the process of determining if an employee poses a real danger to the workplace is one of the most troublesome challenges facing the employer. This chapter, therefore, is devoted to answering the following questions:

- When is it necessary to have a professional perform a violence risk assessment of an employee?
- What are the goals of the assessment, and how are they achieved?
- If my concern is that the employee may be dangerous, how can I involve him in the process of assessment?
- How do I find the right expert to perform the violence risk assessment?

When Is a Professional Risk Assessment Necessary?

It may be necessary to have a professional perform a violence risk assessment of an employee when any of the following conditions exist:

- When it has been determined that a threat has been made
- When others are threatened by an employee's behavior that is related to violence, such as displaying a weapon or making repeated references to violence
- When behavioral changes are observed under circumstances where there is reason to think that someone is being pushed, such as discipline, possible job loss, or other significant life stressors

It bears saying again that one must proceed with diligence but also with caution. Although any of these conditions may provide a reason for requiring an assessment, they can all just as easily become the basis of a witch hunt! There are no hard and fast rules or foolproof guidelines for knowing the difference. The key is the *process* that you follow in responding to a report or a complaint. As an employer, your responsibility is two-sided. On the one side, you must be diligent, consistent, and prompt in responding to any possible danger. On the other, you must be careful to respect and protect the rights and dignity of an employee drawn into any actions that you take in response to a report. As described in Chapter 9, the two sides balance one another. This balance should be reflected in the policies and procedures that you have developed to ensure a fair, deliberate, and intelligent process of fact finding and decision making.

If you have determined that a risk exists, you should have a professional evaluate the employee at risk. However, the assessment of violence risk is not limited to an examination of one employee to determine whether he presents a danger to others. To be useful, the assessment must take in a wider array of information and issues.

What Are the Goals of the Assessment?

If you have arranged it properly, the assessment will do the following:

1. *Determine if someone is a risk to himself or others.* Answering this question is primarily the job of the violence expert, and it will rarely yield a "yes or no" answer. I often use the "traffic light" analogy to explain to employers how the question can be usefully answered with respect to the appropriate response. These classifications often do not come in pure form, but they are useful as guides to action.[1]

- *Red light*: There is imminent danger that the individual will carry out a plan to harm others. This determination will usually be accompanied by a recommendation to contact law enforcement, arrange for surveillance, warn possible targets, and secure the facility.
- *Yellow light*: There is no immediate risk, but there is a clear potential for violence. It will be necessary to take steps to reduce or remove the risk. The assessment should at least begin to specify the cause of the risk and point to actions needed to reduce or remove the risk. The assessment will warn that if no such action is taken, the situation could worsen and become more acutely dangerous.
- *Green light*: There is no danger of violence. Some stressor or circumstance is causing this concern about violence, but there is no current risk and no indication that even a worsening of the situation would create a risk of violence. A green light situation is sometimes the result of a misunderstanding or a misperception of an employee's behavior. Sometimes it is the result of an error in judgment or a form of manipulative or dysfunctional behavior that verges on threat. This means that even in the absence of an actual risk, the employer may still have to take action in response to unacceptable behavior on the part of the employee in question.

2. *Determine the reason for the threatening or violent behavior.* As we discussed in Chapter 3, violence results from the interaction of person, situation, and setting. To be useful, the assessment process must go beyond looking at the individual alone and explore the interpersonal, familial, and organizational context of the crisis. For example, although the assessment may indicate that the employee has a low flashpoint and a worrisome history of violent behavior, it may also point to poor labor relations that have raised tensions and thwarted communication and problem solving in that employee's unit. It may indicate that diversity-based conflict issues play a part in the eruption of violence or threat. It may uncover severe marital, health, or financial troubles that have driven the person past his ability to cope. Naturally, the results of these explorations will point to very different solutions and actions.

3. *Point toward a course of action.* These discoveries are just as important as those involving the qualities in the person that predispose to violence because they will point specifically to the action or actions to be taken, whether they involve changes at the workplace or interventions to address the non-work-related issues, whether or not they are related to violence risk. It will, for example, help the employer decide between solutions such as moving the employee to another work location, correcting management practices, or arranging for a medical or disability leave, a retirement, discipline or termination, or some combination of these. A comprehensive assessment will thus first determine the level of violence risk, then uncover the causes for the violence or the crisis itself, and finally point to the appropriate action to be taken.

What Is the Process?

The threat-of-violence assessment is a process of information gathering and decision making. The process proceeds by steps, depending on the information developed at each step.

Determination of Risk

When a possible threat is brought to your attention, the first question that needs to be answered is: Is anyone in immediate danger? The employer must immediately gather facts that apply to this question: Has a weapon been displayed? Has a clear intent or plan been expressed? Does the person have the means to do it? How imminent is the threat? If there is an immediate danger, emergency measures must be taken to ensure safety. This may include actions such as contacting law enforcement, securing the facility, notifying potential targets, and arranging for surveillance of the employee who has made threat.

When no immediate danger exists, a crucial task still remains for the employer. A concern about violence *has* been raised; therefore, you must (a) determine what, if any, level of risk exists and (b) determine how to respond to the worrisome or possibly unacceptable behavior.

Administrative Handling of the Employee

Standard modes of discipline and health assessment will not help you here. A number of the cases in this book show clearly how simply suspending the threatening person can seriously disrupt the process of fact finding and ultimate resolution. For the crucial assessment step to be successful, it is essential that the bond between the employer and employee be preserved. With respect to discipline, therefore, it is generally preferable to defer decisions about possible disciplinary actions and simply to remove the employee from the workplace with pay while your investigation is underway. This avoids immediate disputes about fairness, as well as any formal dispute process if a union is present. As an employer, you are making no guarantees about what you will do ultimately about discipline or other administrative actions. You are simply establishing a "time-out" period in which all parties can engage in fact finding and decision making. This was a crucial component in helping the Postal Service establish effective methods of responding to violence issues. For that employer in particular, deferring formal discipline allowed the union to participate with management in fact finding, rather than being forced to oppose management by disputing the disciplinary action (a course that proved disastrous in several cases). The approach that is still most common in our workplaces—suspension pending examination by a doctor—also tends to make the employee feel that he is "fighting for his job." Feeling threatened and embattled, the employee will comply, but he will not be honest about what is really going on for him. The use of an interim, nonpunitive administrative status allows the employee to engage in the process as an participant rather than as an adversary.

Involvement of the Employee

It is crucial that the employer maintain the maximum connection to the employee who is threatening or whose behavior is of concern. The majority of cases will involve reports or allegations of threats rather than an acute violent outbreak or imminent risk. It will involve asking questions and investigating rather than reacting quickly to neutralize a dangerous situation. You do not want to lose the employee by overreacting and making assumptions. As soon as the situation comes to your attention, include him in the process of assessing the level of risk.

If the employer arranges the assessment correctly, the process itself will deescalate the danger. The employee himself should feel himself to be an active, willing participant in the process of violence risk assessment. The most serious— and most common—mistake employers make in these cases is to distance the employee by "sending him" for an assessment by a doctor outside the work environment. This is done mostly out of a fear, almost always mistaken, that confronting the employee directly will "push him over the edge" and escalate the crisis. Nothing could be further from the truth. As discussed in Chapter 3, the person threatening violence is usually someone who has been frustrated in his attempts to make himself visible and establish contact with others. He craves contact and a hearing above all else.

The report of a possible threat presents the employer with an important opportunity to establish direct contact with the employee. In fact, the first person or persons the employee should meet in this process is not a doctor but his own manager, perhaps along with a middle manager or a human resources staff member. At this meeting, the employee should be informed specifically why he is there and how the process will unfold. If there is to be an assessment of violence risk by a professional, the contact with the professional should be explained and demystified and the ground rules set forth. Once the employee is reassured that no decision about discipline or other actions will be made until the conclusion of fact finding and assessment, the process of assessment should be explained to him. This will include a full disclosure about how the assessment will be used and the limits of confidentiality (see "Policy Guidelines for Violence Assessments," below).

The employer who follows these guidelines wins on several counts. If you approach the employee in a firm but collaborative way, communicate an "innocent before proven guilty" attitude, and do not move immediately to discipline, the employee will feel trusting enough to enter into an assessment. His first contact in this process is with you, the employer, at the worksite, rather than in an unfamiliar medical or office setting removed from you and from the decision-making process. He will feel that he is participating in a neutral and open investigation process, of which his meeting with a professional is but one part. In this way, the bond between employer and employee is not broken; in fact, it may be reinforced. This may be true even when the ultimate result is the employee's separation from the workplace! (See chapter 7.)

Specialized Assessment Model

It is crucial for the success of any response to a threat-of-violence crisis that the process not be "given over" to an outside professional but that it be fully owned by the employer. When an employee threatens violence, or when there is a concern about possible violence, it is crucial that the employer maintain complete control over the process at every step. Several steps will ensure this:

Team Action

Through a team approach, make decisions about each step based on information from a range of sources. The professional assessment is an important source, but only one among others. Depending on the nature of the situation, there will be an ongoing need for coordination and teamwork between human resources, security, legal, and health and safety departments, the manager of the employee in question, and management of the affected or potentially affected work units.

Finding the Right Professional

Not any mental health professional will do. Here is an all-too-common scenario. Imagine that you have a report of a threat and an employee ready for an assessment. You call up Dr. Smith, a local psychologist with a good reputation, who says, in response to your request, "Sure, send him over to my office. I'll meet with him and then give you my opinion." *Keep looking!* This is not the expert you want! The violence assessment is accomplished through the gathering of information from multiple sources (Fein et al., 1995). Some of this information will come directly from the workplace. One of the necessary qualifications for the professional is an understanding of workplace issues and a willingness and ability to deal with people in the context of their work environment. It is crucial that he or she work closely with you in the process of information gathering. The expert you *do* want

- will ask to talk with you and with other employees in the work setting who may have relevant information
- will ask to see medical and personnel records
- will be willing to come on site if that facilitates his or her access to records and his or her meetings with you and other staff
- will understand that his or her work will be incomplete and not useful unless this collateral information is part of his or her data gathering

- will understand the need to obtain informed consent from the employee so that information can be shared in a legal and consensual fashion

Do not wait until the crisis is upon you to begin your search for the expert who can provide this service. Find someone who is open to working with you and who understands and agrees on the methods and the ground rules concerning information gathering and information sharing. The expert you are looking for will most likely be a psychologist or a psychiatrist. He or she may have credentials as a forensic specialist, which indicates experience with legal matters involving criminal behavior or competency to stand trial. These credentials may be relevant to your needs, but do not rely on them exclusively in your search for an expert to help you with these situations. Familiarity with violence is an important qualification, but familiarity, comfort, and expertise with workplace-related issues is just as critical. In fact, mental health professionals called on by employers in threat-of-violence cases are not helpful when they apply traditional models that are not suited to the assessment of violence risk in a workplace context.

The Limits of Standard Mental Health and Occupational Medicine Approaches for the Assessment of Violence Risk

Several standard occupational health approaches are most typically applied in cases of threat of violence or suspicion of violent potential. It will be useful to look at these standard mental health assessment approaches because each brings its own problems, limitations, and risks when applied to the issue of threat of violence.

The "Counseling" Approach

Often, the mental health consultant, psychologist, or Employee Assistance Program (EAP) provider receives the following request: "Our employee has been making threatening statements of late. He seems unhappy with his job, and we think he is under too much stress. Can you give him some counseling?" Whenever I hear this, I ask, "What makes you think he needs counseling?" It is possible that some form of mental health intervention may be required or helpful at some point. However, the first step must be to understand what is going on in the context of the job environment. It is pointless, for example, to offer supportive counseling to someone when part of the problem is that he has never before been confronted with the unacceptability of his bullying or intimidating behavior. Appropriate limit setting might have solved the problem a long time ago, and it might solve it now. It is useful and wise for an employer to facilitate access to mental health counseling for employees. But in the case of threat of violence, safety, not treatment, is the first job of the employer. It is just as unfair and potentially injurious to the possible offender for the employer to ignore or tolerate unacceptable or potentially danger-ous behavior as it would be to discriminate against him because of a mental or behavioral disability. If a person is at risk for injurious behavior, limiting the response to a referral for counseling—for example, through the EAP—could be considered an insufficient and even negligent response. Similarly, it is pointless, wrong, and potentially costly to suggest to an employee that she be treated for stress when she is being abused by her supervisor or is struggling with unacceptable working conditions. It is the employer's job to first determine whether there are causes underlying the threat that may be the responsibility of the workplace and under its control.

Employers commonly make the mistake of automatically turning to the EAP to assist in the assessment of a threat of violence. Many EAPs are not equipped or skilled to provide this service. Furthermore, involvement in this process may compromise the role and image of the EAP as a confidential counseling service completely removed from disciplinary or other administrative functions of the employer. EAPs do have an important role in the overall violence prevention program, however. If there is an EAP service, the counselor should be involved as a team member in program planning and in helping the employer to identify specialists with the needed skills. EAP professionals can also be involved in initial information gathering and decision making when a workplace-based situation is reported. Fundamentally, however, confusing the assessment of dangerousness with a counseling or mental health function is a form of "medicalizing" the problem. Threatening or violent behavior is not *necessarily* indicative of mental illness. We grant mental health professionals too much power when we assume that they can handle this kind of problem simply through the exercise of their professional expertise.[2]

The "Fitness-for-Duty" Approach

When illness or injury forces someone to leave the workplace, the employer requires a "fitness-for-duty" (FFD) evaluation to determine when someone has recovered sufficiently to return to work. Typically, the FFD is a medical assess-ment, carried out by company medical staff or an outside contractor, to determine a return-to-work date and to specify temporary or permanent limitations on future work functioning. Employers also use the procedure to evaluate someone's psychological fitness in the case of mental illness or problems related to emotional stress when this interferes with job performance, and this is an appropriate use of the process. However, the FFD is increasingly being called into service to determine if someone suspected of dangerous or threatening behavior can safely remain in the workplace or return to work after being removed because of threatening behavior. The FFD is not appropriate or useful for this purpose. In cases of threat of violence, job performance is not the question. Rather, the question is the far more complex and high-stakes issue of whether the person is a danger to himself or others. When you ask for a FFD, that is what you get: an opinion about a person's ability to work. That is not the question that is being asked when violence is the issue.

The processes of information gathering and decision making also differ radically for a threat of violence and for a standard work injury or illness situation. As we discussed above, to assess the risk of violence, you must go beyond an examination of the individual and into the collection of several kinds of collateral information. The employer must be sure to gather enough information from a wide enough range of sources to ensure that he or she understands not only the situation of the individual but the total context in which the presumed threat has happened. In contrast, the FFD is an administrative procedure that has bearing on the employment status of an individual. It is governed by standard policies governing benefits (how a person is compensated for time off the job), discipline if it is a matter of having broken the rules, job accommodation if a temporary or permanent disability is involved, or reimbursement from a third party (i.e., an insurance company) for medical treatment. Some of these issues may become important eventually, but they must not be allowed to structure the initial response to the threat. It is inappropriate, for example, given the urgency of the situation and the context of the assessment, to pursue reimbursement from a third party for the expenses of a threat assessment. The prudent employer who wishes to obtain accurate information through a neutral process will suspend questions of fitness and employment status until the circumstances of the alleged threat are determined. In short, one must not mix questions of occupational health, disability, job status, and reimbursement with the need to assess a possible threat of violence.

The Standard Psychiatric Exam

Like the FFD, a standard psychiatric examination is a general procedure designed to address a broad spectrum of questions about emotional and cognitive functioning. Asked to examine an individual, a psychiatrist or other mental health professional such as a psychologist or clinical social worker will take a "snapshot" intended to quickly answer a handful of crucial questions, including: Is the person capable of functioning adequately in the world with respect to his thinking and emotional control? Is he in touch with reality (e.g., does he think he is a famous figure, or is he hearing voices commanding him to commit certain acts)? Is he so depressed or anxious that he cannot carry on everyday tasks at home and at work? Is he organized enough in his thinking to able to care for himself on an everyday basis? Finally and most important, is he a danger to himself or others?

The psychiatrist has a limited amount of time. If he is confronted with an individual sent by an employer, he will attempt to get those immediate questions answered and report his results. He may go beyond that if the employer is asking more specific questions because of what has happened. For example, if the employer says, "This man has threatened his supervisor, and we want to know if he is dangerous," the psychiatrist will be sure to ask the employee about his violent feelings or intentions. The psychiatrist will try to determine if the employee has an actual plan to hurt his supervisor and if he has the means to carry out his plan. He or she will determine if there is a history of violence.[3] He or she will attempt to understand why the employee might be motivated to be violent and will attempt to determine if this is a person who impulsively acts out physically or if he is someone who can think about consequences, control himself, and find other ways to deal with frustration or anger. The psychiatrist may try to determine if this is someone with a firm sense of right and wrong or if he is someone who readily tramples on the rights and safety of others. All these are important, relevant questions for a psychiatrist to address when confronted with the task of evaluating someone suspected of violence potential, and the competent professional will attempt to answer them. But he or she is operating within the context of the standard, medical model clinical interview. This limits him in several crucial ways.

The Context of the Examination

The practitioner's findings are based only on what the employee reports and on the practitioner's observations of the employee. Both will be influenced by the context. How is the doctor perceived by the employee who is being examined? Is he or she seen as someone there to help or as someone who is in league with the company that is trying to persecute the employee? Is this examination seen as a test that the employee must pass to clear his name and save his job? Failing any alternative arrangements or understandings, this is the context in which the examination will occur, and it will limit the value of the information that the practitioner can glean. The employee will most likely defend his actions or completely deny the allegations. Most important, he will omit or minimize the actual distress that he may be suffering; no one wants a sick, overstressed employee! Further complicating the picture, whenever there is an issue of questionable or problematic supervision or management practices, many employees will be quite forthcoming with their complaints. The doctor, hearing this tale of woe, will humanely "take the side" of the employee, sympathizing with him about his mistreatment at the hands of his employer. But what is needed here is an objective evaluator, not an advocate for an employee who may have been wronged. The psychiatrist or psychologist's ability to be helpful is severely compromised when he or she is drawn into the struggle between the employee and the employer. However, without adequate information from the employer about the total context of the situation, this becomes a real risk. I have seen this happen too many times.

Information

No matter how skilled practitioners are, they are limited by these factors in determining the risk because they do not have information that tells them about the context in which the alleged threat has occurred. They have not spoken to other employees about the employee or his alleged threats. They have not consulted with the employer or looked at employment records. They have no sense about what is going on in the workplace with respect to changes, stressors, or other relevant conditions. Behavior takes place in a context. A snapshot of the person's mental functioning is just that, and only that.

Agreements and Understandings
About Exchange of Information

Standard medical and mental health practice is governed by laws of privacy as well as professional ethics involving patient-doctor confidentiality. These all limit, even to the point of prohibiting, the communication of the results of examinations to anyone besides the patient. Much confusion and misunderstanding exists about this when an employer is acting to preserve workplace safety. Many employers, with an almost naive timidity, assume that their access to information is limited because that is what they are used to. *In the absence of prior and specific agreements worked out for these kinds of situations with practitioners, these standard confidentiality practices will prevail.* They will seriously handicap the effort to answer the crucial question: Is there danger here? To be prepared, therefore, the employer should consider the following policy guidelines to direct specialized assessments for dangerousness.

Policy Guidelines for Violence Assessments

The most important fact to keep in mind is that the dangerousness assessment is *not* a standard psychiatric or mental health assessment. Because the assessment is required for special circumstances involving a possible safety or health hazard in the workplace, procedures and policies apply that are different from those that may apply to a standard mental health assessment or treatment scenario. The following guidelines should be written into a document and an agreement should be obtained from any professionals who provide this service for the company or agency.

Informed Consent

The usual rules governing doctor-patient confidentiality will not apply in a case where an employer requires an assessment of an employee's possible dangerousness. The employee must be informed by the employer, and again by the mental health professional, that this assessment has been requested by the employer because of concerns about harm to self or others and that information pertaining to that question will be shared with the employer. There should be a written form to that effect signed by the employee.

Content and Scope of the Report

The employee should also be informed that any verbal communication or written report from the provider will be restricted to information pertaining to the question being asked by the employer—for example, the presence, nature, and extent of the threat, conditions that affect the level of the threat, suitability to return to work, and recommendations for treatment or possible changes in the employment situation. Information about the employee that does not bear on the issue of threat or safety or that does not bear on the employee's ability to function in the workplace will not be communicated to the employer *in any form*. This includes information about any medical or psychiatric diagnosis or past or present treatment for any medical or mental condition that does not pertain to the specific situation.

In other words, if it does not apply to the question of dangerousness, it is not the employer's business!

Communication

Following the assessment, the provider may convey findings verbally, to be followed by a written report if requested. The employer should designate specific contacts for the provider. These should be as limited as possible. They may include the health and safety manager, the EAP, or another designee from human resources, security, or legal departments. *It must be clear to the provider that he or she is not to discuss the case with anyone else.* In cases where an employee has engaged legal help or is involved with other agencies in the community, and information is requested from the provider as part of a legal action or other request for services, the provider should agree to inform the employer of this request, or of any other contact with the employee or his agent, before carrying out any discussions or sharing information with another party.

Employee's Access

The employee should have access to the report on request. The procedures would be similar to those governing access to any other employment-related records. The provider should write the report with this in mind.

Know Your Questions

Evaluation is the first order of business when violence is in question. Important questions must be addressed to clarify the history and context of the problem at hand—for example: Where is the record of discipline for past problems? Where is the documentation of performance problems or claims for medical disability? What is the history of changes, morale issues, or complaints in the work unit? What do you know about what else may be going on in the employee's life? In other words, what is the total administrative and psychosocial context of this behavior? Until these questions are addressed, no violence risk assessment can be considered complete or reliable, and any treatment prescription, intervention, or decision about administrative action is premature.

Assemble your team, know your expert, involve your employee, and proceed with compassion and caution.

Notes

1. I learned this formulation from my colleague Steven White, PhD.

2. Labig (1995) offers a good discussion of the relationship of mental illness to violence, taking on the "myth of a violent personality type."

3. Robert Fein (personal communication, 1998) cautions against the conventional wisdom that a history of violence is a reliable predictor. His study of attacks on public figures reveals that fewer than 25% of the attackers had histories of arrests for violent crime (Fein & Vossekuil, 1998).

12

Seven Steps to Workplace Violence Prevention

What we believe precedes policy and practice.

Max DePree, *Leadership Is an Art*

Here it is: the chapter at the end that promises to condense the entire book into one short, easy-to-absorb package. Perhaps you looked at the table of contents and came directly here. Go ahead! Skip right to this chapter, and then go back through the book to fill in the details. What follows is a series of steps: Each one depends on what comes before. If you follow the process outlined below, you will achieve your goal of preventing violence from disrupting your workplace, damaging the lives and health of your employees, and compromising your effectiveness as a manager. In undertaking this process, you will embark on a journey in which you will learn a great deal about the values of your company, the quality of your leadership team, and the capacity of your entire organization for growth and change. The steps are the following:

- Get support from the top.
- Form a team.
- Perform a workplace violence risk audit.
- Develop policies and procedures.
- Conduct training in the policy and procedures.
- Arrange for easy, nonpunitive access to medical and mental health expertise.
- Have clear, commonsense policies and procedures for terminations and layoffs.

Step 1: Get Support From the Top

The entire process of developing a violence prevention capacity—from the risk audit, through team formation, to policy development, through training and implementation—can be accomplished effectively only with the visible support and participation of the top level of company (and union) leadership. This support is expressed in two crucial and very concrete ways.

Team Appointment

The first indication of support is the assignment of the team. The team will guide the process from design to initiation to ongoing implementation. It must be composed of people in leadership positions who are empowered to make decisions. A team like this can only be assembled with the direction and support of someone near the top of the organization. When I see a single middle-level person from a safety or a training function burdened with the task of developing a policy or a training program, I suspect that the entire effort will come to nothing. This is often a sign of a lack of support or only passing support from the top.

Culture Change

Implementing a successful violence prevention program requires culture change, often of a profound nature. It is likely to require alterations in time-honored practices in areas such as labor relations, injury management, and other human resource procedures. But no one is going to change the way things are done unless there is a clear message that this is truly the intention and desire of leadership at the highest level. Visible participation from the top of the organization helps ensure that the program will not become another set of rules or procedures that are never followed. The best designed and conceived training program will fail to produce change in the absence of visible, tangible support from the highest levels.

Step 2: Form a Team

The team is composed of stakeholders representing a range of functions. Depending on how these particular jobs are structured in your organization, they should include health and safety, legal, human resources, labor relations/employee relations, employee assistance, union, and operations personnel. Keeping in mind the principle of involvement from the top, a high-ranking executive should be on the team, actively in the beginning, and then perhaps *ex officio* once the program is launched.[1]

Once appointed, the team will first design the audit process and then develop the policy. This team will thus grow and evolve along with the process and will maintain responsibility for the program over time. After the policy has been crafted and roles have been defined, the team, with its top management members, will design and take part in the training sessions. Once the program is underway, designated members will receive and process requests for assistance and reports of tension or threat. Over time, the group will continue to oversee the program and take responsibility for reviewing its effectiveness.

Step 3: Perform a Workplace Violence Risk Audit

Workplace violence comes in many forms, as described in Chapter 3. No two companies will face the same combination of threat from people outside the workplace or from within. Furthermore, factors such as physical security setup, organizational structure and culture, and existing policies will all affect the way in which employees are exposed to various violence risks. To craft a useful policy, therefore, you must determine your organizational violence risk profile. The results of a companywide audit will provide specific data about past experience, current exposures, and possible warning signs. An audit can be structured in a variety of ways, but it should include components that will provide the following information:

- *Employee opinions and concerns.* This information can be obtained through some combination of written surveys, interviews, and groups. I am partial to focus groups facilitated by outside consultants. These groups tend to yield the fullest, most candid picture of employees' fears and vulnerabilities. Focus groups also reveal the best information about what the important system issues are, such as safety or security concerns, labor management problems, or diversity.

- *Past experience with violence and conflict.* Interviews with key people and records reviews will yield not only the frequency and kind of incidents but the stories behind these occurrences. How did the episode begin (warning signs heard or not heard)? How did your system respond (well or not well)? This inquiry is likely to yield important data for the process of policy and procedure development to come.

- *Current policies and systems* that relate to your violence prevention capability. You will see what policies are missing and what existing structures and procedures may need to be modified.

Step 4: Develop Policies and Procedures

Once your team has processed the information from the organizational audit, it can set about developing the policy. Sample policies are easy to come by—there is one included at the end of this book—and they can help set out the basic form of the policy. The formula is simple and sensible. It differs little from a standard sexual harassment policy: (a) Define workplace violence, (b) set out a "zero-tolerance" standard and the range of specific consequences, (c) specify the reporting procedures, and (d) ensure safety and nonretaliation for reporters. It is up to the team to fill in the blanks with the specific list of behaviors and situations that will come under the policy as well as with the procedures that the company will follow.

It should be clear that you cannot publish a policy until you have accomplished Steps 1 through 3. Without support from the top, there will not be an effective team. Without an audit of some kind, the policy will not reflect the specific violence risks the company is facing, the behaviors it wants to track, or the actual procedures that will work for the organization.

Step 5: Conduct Training in the Policy and Procedures

The purpose of training is to ensure the implementation of the policy and the procedures that support it. It is not, as some assume, to give your employees the ability to predict or spot dangerousness. The policy is the heart of a *system of coordinated response* that depends on the participation of your employees. It is essential that your people, especially your first-line managers (and stewards if there is a union), provide the early notification that allows the system to function most effectively. The worst workplace violence cases in my experience began with a manager's failing to bring the situation to attention of people at the proper levels early enough. Individual managers, at any level, should not be making judgment calls about these issues. However, that is precisely what will happen unless you convey a clear message that any possible warning signs must be reported so that an appropriate process of fact finding and response can take place.

Here is where the culture change begins to happen. Many corporate cultures discourage reporting. This is usually for one or both of the following reasons: (a) Managers have been trained to handle things on their own and to not bother superiors with problems, and (b) some workplace cultures tolerate or normalize conflictual and threatening behavior. I recall standing before a group of postal employees as part of a violence training team consisting of managers and union officers. A letter carrier in the back of the room angrily related how he had attempted to report that he had witnessed another carrier threatening a fellow worker with violence. The supervisor to whom he reported it said to him: "Well, let me know if anything happens." We do not know why that supervisor responded in that way (perhaps he thought it was acceptable for employees to threaten one another, or perhaps he disliked or disbelieved the reporter). We do know, however, that by the time the training session was over, every manager in the room had been put on notice that to fail to act on a report like that would now be unacceptable and would even subject them to discipline. I have another vivid memory from a similar Postal Service training session that took place in a large mail-sorting facility. A young clerk sat quietly in the back of the room as we explained how a team composed of union and management members would now be available to respond to violence and behavioral issues. Identifying himself as a union steward, the young man raised his hand and asked, "Do you mean that I could actually call on this team to help with this kind of situation?" He then went on to say that he had been dealing with an employee, a member of the union, who had been acutely suicidal for months. The steward had not felt that he could go anywhere in the system with his concerns about this because, in his words, "It might have hurt the guy's job security."

The policy is there to put an end to the kind of risky behavior illustrated by these stories. Each component of your prevention program supports the other. You cannot have an effective team response unless employees understand the importance of early reporting. At the same time, you cannot require employees to report signs of trouble unless you have established a system that is reliable and safe. The primary goal of your training is to ensure that employees at every level are willing to make a phone call *even when they are in doubt* about what to do. They must learn that on the other end of that phone is a process that will take the decision making and judgment calls out of their hands and into the hands of a corporate-level team that will ensure fairness and safety for everyone involved. Employees at every level must understand that participation in this process is the correct—and required— thing to do whenever there is a question of violence or self-harm.

Step 6: Arrange for Easy, Nonpunitive Access to Medical and Mental Health Expertise

It is essential that the process of dangerousness assessment and threat investigation not be tied to discipline or other administrative action or to a standard work injury or health claim process. Standard procedures for assessing job-linked health conditions are not only inappropriate for handling threats or dangerousness but possibly dangerous and destructive to the process itself. As discussed in detail in Chapter 11, a threat-of-violence assessment has different goals than these standard occupational health activities. Whereas the purpose of a standard assessment is to determine whether someone is fit to do his or her job, the goal here is to find out if someone is dangerous and, if not, to determine the nature of the problem.

The way the assessment is handled is perhaps the linchpin of the entire process of responding to a threat of violence. As a number of the cases in this book demonstrate vividly, failing to prepare for this step can subvert the entire process, bringing disastrous consequences. If, on the other hand, you have carefully selected a professional and have worked out your procedures carefully, you will be able to proceed assured of two critical elements: (a) The employee will feel comfortable and open about entering into the assessment process, and (b) you will have *immediate and legal* access to critical information about dangerousness. Don't neglect this step!

Step 7: Have Clear, Commonsense Policies and Procedures for Terminations and Layoffs

Most of the calls that we receive requesting help with threats of violence are from employers contemplating a layoff or faced with a termination that is making them nervous. The two events seem to be inextricably linked in the minds of managers: *Job loss equals violence.* And there is wisdom in this connection. We can all easily associate losing our job with our deepest fears: humiliation, isolation, loss of physical support. Because these fears and experiences can indeed lead to severe breakdown and violence in some people, it is important to be prepared to handle these events wisely and carefully.

Termination for Cause: The Time It Takes

The return of the fired employee to exact murderous revenge has become the symbol of Americans' fear of workplace violence, despite what statistics may tell us about the actual probability that this will occur in one's own work setting. This fear accurately represents the rage and insecurity that pervades a workplace in the throes of change or a community struggling with economic contraction. Job loss, even for the most vulnerable of individuals, however, need not spell danger. *No one ever took revenge simply for being fired.* Employees who become threatening always talk about *the way they were made to feel* in the process of losing their jobs.[2] In my experience, one factor in particular increases the risk of violence or threat connected with a termination: the length of time that elapses between the actions that led to the termination and the termination itself.[3]

Believe it or not, this period is often *years,* and it is a major risk factor. This is because what usually happens between the time the behavior is first noticed and the employer finally acts has not helped the employee and the employer move toward a resolution of the problem (Chapter 4 of this book furnishes a grim example). Typically, an employer will come to us about someone who has reportedly threatened others or who is perceived as dangerous. In these cases, we usually find that there is a long history of problematic behavior and performance issues. Although intimidating, harassing, and even threatening behavior has been going on for months and often years, there is little, if any, documentation of administrative actions taken in response to these behaviors. This is because most threatening behavior is used to control and intimidate others, and it usually works. In the absence of company policies regarding violence and threats, this sort of behavior is often ignored: The offender is given a "wide berth." When the person finally pushes too far, the company managers are in a weak position because they have ignored or tolerated the behavior for so long. This is not good for the offender and not good for the company. When employees belong to a union and disciplinary or corrective actions are subject to a collective bargaining agreement, there is an added delay.

Have your policies governing threatening and violent behavior be specific, clear, and consistently applied, and document all actions carefully. When there is a reported threat, you should be able to open a file and see if there is a record of previous actions taken in response to behaviors in violation of the zero-tolerance policy or other rules pertaining to conduct, safety, or health. If, in the course of your response to a incidence of unacceptable behavior, your investigation turns up information relevant to violence risk (e.g., a history of violence, problems with alcohol, or experience with and ownership of weapons), this can now properly, usefully, and legally become the basis for any action. It is not a good idea to drag this process out. Giving the person "another chance" without taking action or exploring the causes for the behavior, or ignoring the behavior out of fear, is clearly inexcusable. Doing so out of compassion is similarly misguided. If a union is present and if union and management collude by passively allowing adversarial, rule-bound procedures to control the process, they are jointly abdicating their responsibility to preserve the safety of the workplace and, not least of all, the safety of the employee himself.

Layoffs: The Need for Special Procedures

The unrelenting forces of organizational change affecting virtually all industrial sectors require that corporate leaders adopt a deliberate, focused approach to violence prevention. This is true for two reasons. First, change creates psychological uncertainty and economic insecurity. These in turn create stress that in some employees results in threatening or violent behavior. Second, as any modern manager will attest, change puts enormous stress on organizations. Systems are in transition, and managers are struggling to adapt to increased responsibilities. In such an environment, rapid and smooth decision making, especially in crisis situations (which proliferate in a change environment), can falter. To be fully prepared for the special risks that accompany organizational change, leaders must take action in three areas:

1. *Communication.* Because of the fears associated with change and uncertainty in a change environment, the need for information is unending. Leaders must be prepared to visibly and actively communicate with employees on a continual basis. Communication includes listening and responding to concerns, not just delivering scripted messages. The risk is that, exhausted by the constant demand for information and the expressions of mistrust from frightened employees, leaders withdraw from listening and discussion.

2. *Organizational transition team.* It is best that a team of leaders, including functions such as human resources, security, safety and health, and employee assistance, be given the task of monitoring the health of the organization throughout the transition period. This team, constantly alert to what is going on in the organization, will be able to respond to needs and crises emerging from the organization on an ongoing basis.

3. *Safety nets.* The actions of a transition team, together with the assurance of continual two-way communication, will provide a safety net for an organization experiencing the stress of change. It is to be expected that work groups and individuals will show signs of stress and occasional breakdown. Concerns about threats and violent climate will surface if there is a listening ear and a reliable response procedure. Frequent information sessions and group support sessions will provide the forum for such concerns. Other functions related to change should also be brought into the loop. For example, in our work recently with a utility company, we arranged to meet regularly with the firm hired to provide outplacement services for displaced employees. Whenever the outplacement staff had a concern about the stability or mental health of one of these people, they contacted the team for consultation. In addition, managers who had to lay off employees were instructed to alert the proper team members when they had concerns about a potentially problematic or dangerous layoff scenario.

Epilogue: A False Crisis?

In October 1994, the *Wall Street Journal* published an article on workplace violence entitled "A False Crisis" (Larsen, 1994). In it, the reporter characterized the fear surrounding workplace homicide as "hysterical." Clearly having done his homework, he pointed to the U.S. statistics that show only 4% of the workplace homicides related to worker-on-worker violence. In my response to the article, I shared the author's dim view of data used in the service of scare tactics and sensationalism. But, as I pointed out, controversy about statistics and exploitation by slick marketers does not add up to a "false crisis."

Don't talk about a false crisis to the thousands of executives, human resources managers, safety directors, and company attorneys who are dealing with increasing regularity with this troubling issue. Don't argue this to the school principal who is wondering if her school will be in the national headlines tomorrow. These people are not thronging to seminars and buying books and videotapes about workplace violence because someone frightened them with survey outcomes or government data. Rather, they are driven by the very real and immediate fear and frustration caused by a problem that is happening to them, every day, in their offices, factories, stores, schools, and daily contacts with the public.

There may not be a murderer lurking in the next cubicle or loading dock. But consider the effect of working in an environment in which conflict, threats, and intimidation replace communication and cooperation. Imagine being a manager or human resources director who must deal with a threat of violence or reports of an employee who is unraveling under stress but who is hamstrung because the only tools available to deal with the crisis are standard disciplinary or disability procedures. Homicides are the tip of the workplace violence iceberg, an iceberg that consists of domestic violence intruding into the workplace, interemployee stalkings, workers at daily risk of armed robbery by criminals, abuse and threat by customers, and threats or harassment by superiors or coworkers. It is an issue that has little to do with arguments about statistics and everything to do with how the workplace can preserve itself as a humane, productive, and stable institution in the face of the violence, desperation, and upheaval that is happening in the world around it.

Preventing violence requires much more than simply publishing a policy or responding to emergencies—it is not about putting out fires. Any emergency or crisis involving a threat or an act of violence requires that learning take place. If your organization has not experienced change or growth as a result of an act of violence, a frightening threat, or a "close call," then you have reinforced your reactive crisis orientation. Where there has been no self-examination, you have fostered powerful, dangerous illusions: "This was an isolated event." "He was a bad apple, but he is gone now." And the conditions that led to the crisis will persist.

The way a corporation, a federal or private agency, a small business, or a town deals with the reality of violence or threats—originating from within or from without—has implications for its very survival. When a threat or act of violence occurs, it is a signal thrown up from the myriad of crises that confront the workplace continually: the stress of families living on increasingly thin ice; the unrelenting pressure of wrenching organizational change and competition on a global scale; a crisis in health care that threatens the availability of mental health care for an enlarging sector of the population; people at risk every day from the societal and political violence that continues to plague our species. If the threat of violence within their walls and intruding into the workplace from the outside moves managers and union leadership to attend to these fundamental issues, then this very real crisis will have provided an opportunity of considerable value.

Notes

1. The importance of stakeholder input in the design phase has been recognized by workers in the field of alternate dispute resolution. Interestingly, one writer also pointed out the importance of CEO involvement in the successful design and implementation of alternate dispute resolution systems; see Rowe (1997).

2. See the discussions in Chapters 5 and 9 on procedural justice and perceptions of fairness. The cases presented in these chapters illustrate this point powerfully.

3. De Becker (1997) offers an excellent discussion of the dangers of protracted or delayed terminations and a list of practical suggestions.

Afterword

s we go to press, shocking public acts of violence continue to thrust the issue of workplace violence into our national consciousness. In early 1998, the shootings of children and teachers by adolescent boys in public schools in two states sent American society into a tailspin of horror and confusion. Later that year, the fatal shooting of two U.S. Capitol police officers in the Capitol Building in Washington, D.C., released a groundswell of grief and outrage. What captured my interest, however, more than the paroxysms of public shock and media attention, was the search for *explanations* that accompanied these events. Within days of the first of the school shootings, President Clinton called for legislation to ban the importing of assault weapons. At the same time, journalists in print editorials and broadcast specials were hauling out the timeworn controversies about the effects of media violence on children and on the culture at large. After the Capitol shootings, when it was revealed that the man accused of the crime had been treated for schizophrenia, the public was barraged with information and opinion on the relationship of violence to mental illness, particularly schizophrenia.

What we see in the reactions to these recent events is the same hunger for quick fixes and simple causes that we observed in many of the cases presented in this book. It is not hard to understand the urgency of this need: Violence affects virtually every kind of workplace, from schools, factories, and offices to retail stores and public buildings, and even the U.S. Capitol. But as I have argued, this is a crisis that cannot be successfully confronted with one-dimensional explanations and convenient objects of blame. The causes of violence are not to be found simply in the availability of guns or the abundance of television violence, or in the mental health history or lifestyle profile of a perpetrator. Rather, they are to be discovered by examining the very fabric of the *systems* in place to respond to violence risk.

When, faced with the terrible spectacle of a schoolyard slaughter, we race to embrace solutions such as weapons control or the limiting of exposure to media violence, we run the very serious risk of ignoring the crucial questions that must be asked about these cases. Where, for example, was the collaboration between school, family, and local law enforcement in the response to the obvious danger signals and cries for help exhibited by these children and their families? When, in the aftermath of a savage, irrational attack at the most venerable of national institutions, we fix on schizophrenia—or any other presumed risk factor, whether combat veteran, gun enthusiast, or Montana-based loner—as the focus for our horror and outrage, we ignore similar questions: How did the systems designed to respond to mental health emergencies, threats, and other forms of aberrant behavior function to signal authorities that a threat may have existed? We must ask here, as in the cases of the school shootings: Did the people in any of these systems *talk* to one another?

In every case analyzed in the preceding chapters, violence was the result of a *series* of events, the last act in a chain of signals. Such signals, however, are received by *different listeners*: In the most recent cases, for example, these listeners included a school administration, schoolmates, neighbors and friends, local police, the FBI, and the mental health unit of a hospital. The signals rarely make sense or add up to a clear warning when the information is not shared among these multiple "listening posts." In the absence of this sharing of information, there is no opportunity to submit the information to rational thought and to an analysis that can lead to effective solutions.

Our responsibility as a society in the aftermath of these events is to reject our tendency to quick fixing, blaming, and witch hunting and to embark instead on the study of what has happened so that we can learn from it. I believe that once we engage in that learning process, what we find will lead to (a) an uncovering, in every case, of multiple warning signals, received by a multiplicity of societal entities, whether familial, community, business, or governmental, and (b) the clear need for coordination and communication between these entities. The results of our learning will point to the need for structures that will ensure communication and coordination between these components of society.

How do we begin to design and develop these cooperative structures? The process will anticipate the solution: The study and learning from these tragic events should be conducted through a collaboration of stakeholders—business, labor, government, and private foundations and groups. The meeting place is not important; it could be the corporate boardroom, union headquarters, or congressional hearing room. What is crucial is that the work begin and that all the players be at the table. In the same way, it should be clear that a plethora of funding sources, both public and private, have a direct interest in this issue and should be tapped.

In the early 1950s, Lewis Mumford, the American social philosopher, historian, and educator, was sorely troubled about the future of Western society. He surveyed the Cold War landscape and was appalled by the prospect of global annihilation. In his book *In the Name of Sanity,* Mumford (1954) issued a passionate plea to humanity to step back from the brink of destruction and embrace world cooperation at every level. It is our blind pursuit of security through a belief in technology, arms, and "isolated efforts alone," he wrote, that distances us from our humanity and that will lead to cataclysm (p. 33). "Help us to see!" he beseeched, quoting from Henry Adams's prayer,

> . . . for it is our unseeingness that has permitted us to stumble so close to the abyss. "Help us to know," for the withholding of knowledge and the reluctance to draw conclusions from the knowledge we do possess add willful ignorance to willful blindness. But above all we must recover that which we have lost through the very techniques of scientific knowledge and invention: the power to feel, which is at the basis of all truly human relationships, for once sympathy, pity and love are withdrawn, intelligence will likewise fail us, and we shall treat other human beings as if they were mere things or objects. . . . Yes, help us to *feel.* Our numbness is our death. . . . We must as a condition for survival, recover our humanity again; the capacity for rational conduct, free from compulsive fears and pathological hatreds; the capacity for love and confidence and cooperation, for humorous self-criticism and disarming humility. (pp. 164-165)

"Our numbness is our death." Our coalitions against violence in our homes, schools, streets, and workplaces must be based on a commitment to overcome the forces of isolation, mistrust, and blindness that allow these tragedies to unfold. To be sure, the extreme acts of bloodshed and savagery, those that capture the headlines, furnish the initial spur to collective action. But only a deep, ongoing commitment to change will provide the awareness, compassion, and courage needed to address the countless everyday tragedies that occur in our factories, offices, grievance hearing rooms, schools, and families.

Appendix A

A Sample Policy

The following sample policy can be modified to reflect the particular violence risks of the workplace, "Team" configuration, management structure, notification procedures, labor agreements, and local laws.

Acme Corporation believes that all employees are entitled to a safe, non-threatening workplace environment. Any form of violence,whether actual or perceived, may be in violation of this policy. This includes, but is not limited to:

- Disruptive, intimidating, threatening, or hostile behavior
- Threats via e-mail or voicemail
- Possession of a weapon (or non-approved weapon in some workplaces)
- Violation of restraining orders
- Fighting
- Verbal abuse
- Stalking
- Sabotage or misuse of equipment or company property
- Any behavior that is perceived as threatening

An employee who believes that he or she has been subjected to or the witness of threatening or intimidating behavior by a fellow employee, a customer, a family member, or someone else, should report such conduct according to the procedure outlined below. Any employee who violates this policy may be subject to disciplinary action, up to and including discharge.

Management Responsibility

Violence, or the threats of violence, whether committed by supervisory or nonsupervisory personnel, is against stated company policy and may be considered unlawful as well. Management is responsible for taking action against threats or acts of violence by company personnel or others, including customers, vendors, family members, or others.

It is management's responsibility to show employees that the company is serious about prohibiting and preventing violence in the workplace.

If a supervisor becomes aware of any action, behavior, or perceived threat that may violate this policy, the supervisor is responsible for immediately contacting a member of the Crisis Management Team or specified contact persons.

Notification Procedure

Any employee may bring a concern about violent or threatening behavior, or a situation perceived as creating a hostile or unsafe work environment, to the attention of (specify contact person). In addition, any of the following may be contacted: Manager of Human Resources, Manager of Security, or Director of Safety. In addition, an employee may contact his or her supervisor or union official.

After the Crisis Management Team has been notified of a complaint, or when it receives knowledge that a situation involving a possible threat of violence exists, the team will undertake a thorough investigation to gather all pertinent facts.

Nonretaliation

This policy prohibits retaliation against any employee who brings a complaint of violent, threatening or intimidating behavior. The employee will not be adversely affected in terms and condition of employment or discriminated against or discharged because of the complaint.

Appendix B

Resources for Further Study

The internet now provides a rich source of information and resources for the study of workplace violence and related issues. No list can be complete, but these sites will provide starting points for further research. Most sites have complete manuals and publications that can be downloaded, and copious links to other sites.

Government Agencies

Office of Personnel Management: http://www.opm.gov (opm/workplace/index/html-ssi)
National Institute for Occupational Health and Safety: http://www.cdc.gov/niosh
National Institute of Justice: http://www.ojp.usdoj.gov/nij/
Occupational Safety & Health Administration: http://www.osha.gov

Private Organizations and Foundations

CMG Associates: http://www.CMGassociates.com
Workplace Solutions: http://www.WPS.org

California Foundation for Improvement of Employer-Employee Relations:
http://www.CFEIR.org

American Federation of State, County and Municipal Employees:
http://www.AFSCME.org

National Alliance for Safe Schools: http://www.safeschools.org

Federation of Public Employees: http://www.AFT.org

Family Violence Prevention Fund: http://www.fvpf.org/workplace/index.html

Nurse Advocate, Nurses and Workplace Violence: http://www.nurseadvocate.org

National Labor Management Association: http://www.nlma.org

Cornell/PERC Institute on Conflict Resolution: http://www.ilr.cornell.edu/icr

Minnesota Center Against Violence and Abuse: http://www.mincava.umn.edu

The William and Flora Hewlett Foundation: http://www.hewlett.org

References

Americans with Disabilities Act, 42 U.S.C. §§ 12101-12113 (1990).

Barab, J. (1996a). Public employees as a group at risk for violence. *Occupational Medicine: State of the Art Reviews, 11,* 257-267.

Barab, J. (1996b). When arbitration is not the answer: The union perspective. In J. Narita (Ed.), *Proceedings of the forty-ninth annual meeting of the National Academy of Arbitrators.* Washington, DC: Bureau of National Affairs.

Baxter, V. K. (1994). Workplace violence in the U.S. Post Office. In V. K. Baxter (Ed.), *Labor and politics in the U.S. Postal Service.* New York: Plenum.

Bell, C. A., Stout, N. A., Bender, T. R., Conroy, C. S., Crouse, W. E., & Myers, J. R. (1990). Fatal occupational injuries in the United States, 1980 through 1985. *Journal of the American Medical Association, 263,* 3047-3050.

Braverman, M. (1992). Post-trauma crisis intervention in the workplace. In J. C. Quick, L. R. Murphy, & J. J. Hurrell (Eds.), *Stress and well being in the workplace.* Washington, DC: American Psychological Association.

Braverman, M. (1993). Controlling stress-related costs in the workplace. *Compensation and Benefits Review, 9*(2), 51-57.

California Occupational Safety and Health Administration. (1995, March). *Guidelines for workplace security.* Sacramento: State of California Division of Occupational Safety and Health.

CUPE survey plots scale of violence in the workplace. (1993, November 18). *Calgary Herald,* p. 1.

De Becker, G. (1997). *The gift of fear.* New York: Little, Brown.

DePree, M. (1989). *Leadership is an art.* New York: Dell.

Fein, R. A., & Vossekuil, B. (1998). *Protective intelligence threat assessment investigations: A guide for state and local law enforcement officials* (Research Rep. NJC No. 170612). Washington, DC: U.S. Department of Justice.

Fein, R. A., Vossekuil, B., & Holden, G. A. (1995, September). *Threat assessment: An approach to prevent targeted violence.* Washington, DC: U.S. Department of Justice, National Institute of Justice.

Gleason, S. E. (Ed.). (1997). *Workplace dispute resolution: Directions for the 21st century.* East Lansing: Michigan State University Press.

Guillart, F. J. (1995). *Transforming the organization.* New York: McGraw-Hill.

Hansen, C. (1969). *Witchcraft at Salem.* New York: George Braziller.

Jenkins, E. L., Layne, L. A., & Kisner, S. M. (1992, May). Homicide in the workplace: The U.S. experience, 1980-1988. *AAOHN Journal, 40,* 215-218.

Karlsen, C. F. (1987). *The Devil in the shape of a woman: Witchcraft in colonial New England.* New York: Vintage.

Labig, C. E. (1995). *Preventing violence in the workplace.* New York: Amacom.

Larsen, E. (1994, October 13). A false crisis: How workplace violence became a hot issue. *Wall Street Journal,* p. A1.

Mantell, M. (1994). *Ticking bombs: Defusing violence in the workplace.* Burr Ridge, IL: Irwin.

Monahan, J. (1981). *The clinical prediction of violent behavior.* Bethesda, MD: U.S. Department of Health and Human Services, National Institutes of Health.

Mumford, L. (1954). *In the name of sanity.* New York: Harcourt, Brace.

National Institute for Occupational Safety and Health. (1993, September). *Alert: Preventing violence in the workplace.* Bethesda, MD: U.S. Department of Heath and Human Services, Public Health Service.

Noer, D. M. (1993). *Healing the wounds.* San Francisco: Jossey-Bass.

Northwest National Life Insurance Company. (1993). *Fear and violence in the workplace.*

Occupational Safety and Health Act, 29 U.S.C. §§ 651-2271 (1971).

Pauchant, T. C., & Mitroff, I. I. (1992). *Transforming the crisis-prone organization: Preventing individual, organizational, and environmental tragedies.* San Francisco: Jossey-Bass.

Rowe, M. (1997). Dispute resolution in the non-union environment. In S. E. Gleason (Ed.), *Workplace dispute resolution.* East Lansing: Michigan State University Press.

Senge, P. M. (1990). *The fifth discipline.* New York: Doubleday.

Shrivastava, P. (1992, August). *Crisis theory/practice: Towards a sustainable future.* Paper presented at the New Avenues for Crisis Management Conference, University of Nevada, Las Vegas.

Skarlicki, D. P., Ellard, J. H., & Kelln, B. R. C. (1998). Third-party perceptions of a layoff: Procedural, derogation, and retributive aspects of justice. *Journal of Applied Psychology, 83,* 119-127.

Toscano, G., & Weber, W. (1995, April). *Violence in the workplace.* Washington, DC: U.S. Department of Labor Statistics.

United States Postal Service vs. the National Association of Letter Carriers, Arbitration Case C7N-4B-D 29760, November 8, 1991.

U.S. Department of Health and Human Services. (1994). Occupational injury deaths of postal workers: United States, 1980-1989. *Morbidity and Mortality Weekly Report, 43*(32), 587-595.

Index

Adams, Henry, 137
Administrative leave, use of, 74
American Public Health Association (APHA), 101
American workplace:
  corporate survival, 8
  environmental crisis, 8
  social solutions for, 8
Americans with Disabilities Act:
  crisis management and, 95, 96
  EAP and, 95
Anita Woodward:
  challenged by employee, 56
  company protection denied, 59
  EAP counseling, 60
  employee performance evaluation, 56
  employee reassignment, 59
  employee unstable medical conditions, 58
  lawsuit lost by, 62
  minority slurs to, 57
  promotion of, 56, 57
  request return of, 61
  resignation by, 60
  threats made to, 57
Assessment models:
  employer ownership of, 115

professional resources selection, 115-116
  team action and, 115
Assessment procedures:
  communication gaps and, 52
  employee communication in, 52
  management vs, 51
  proper actions in, 52
Assessment process:
  corporate role in, 82-83
  See also Risk assessments; Risk determination; Warning signs
Auden, W. H., 1

Bank mortgage department:
  critical decision points, 79-81
  employees at, 72-73, 73-74
  evaluation results, 77-78
  lessons learned, 78-79
  management recommendations, 76-77
  profile characteristics, 72
  situation at, 70-72
  summary of, 81-83
  violent employee confrontation, 72
  violent employee meetings, 74-76

About the Author

Mark Braverman, PhD, is a pioneer in the field of traumatic stress in the workplace. In 1985, he and Susan Braverman developed the first comprehensive plan for responding to traumatic events in the workplace for Digital Equipment Corporation. This groundbreaking plan served as model for subsequent work in traumatic stress in the workplace and was the basis for the founding of Crisis Management Group, Inc., in 1988. Dr. Braverman was a founding member of the Harvard University Psychological Trauma Center and served as Instructor in Psychology at Harvard University Medical School from 1987 through 1990. He established the Taskforce on Workplace Trauma for the International Society for Traumatic Stress Studies. He served on the Mental Health Committee for the American College of Occupational and Environmental Medicine. He has lectured, trained, and consulted widely to businesses, federal and state agencies, and academic and professional groups nationally and internationally. He has lectured before the National Institute of Occupational Safety and Health (NIOSH) on the growing problem of workplace violence and before federal agency employer groups in three states on how to protect their workforce from this hazard. He conducts workshops and symposia for the American College of Occupational and Environmental Medicine and the American Psychological Association. In 1992, he testified before a joint congressional subcommittee on the causes of violence in the U.S. Postal Service. He was on the advisory panel of experts for the

Northwestern National Life Insurance Company's groundbreaking survey of workplace stress. He serves as senior trainer and consultant for Workplace Solutions, a project of the Cornell University School of Industrial Relations. He is currently teaching a course on occupational stress at the Harvard University Division of Continuing Studies. He has published over 30 articles and book chapters in academic texts, trade journals, and international symposia on the subjects of workplace trauma intervention, the causes and prevention of workplace violence, and occupational mental health.